U0037477

Authored and Photographed by Wong How Man

CULTURE IN MY THOUGHT

文化
所思

黃效文

著

序

好奇心和良知驅使 *HM* 前進到千年來情勢緊繃的地方。透過他攝影家的眼睛，我們看到了他在世界角落所看到的，和正在發生的改變；透過他探索新聞的觸角，我們也跟著他發掘那些萌芽或消失中的問題。他將我們這些讀者帶進他的探險世界，我不禁好奇，我們這些人到底有沒有像他那樣的洞察力和體力與冰雪中最後一位馴鹿牧人交心、復育純種的緬甸貓、定位依洛瓦底江的源頭、紀錄消失中的巴塔克族。而近期 *HM* 更拓展他的目光遠到義大利的製琴師，提醒我們改變不僅在自然界裡發生。

HM 從不斷論。他觀察，學習。他教導——他希望可以影響下個世代，讓他們有條不紊地探索、記錄事實，讓更多的讀者，像我們這樣坐在沙發裡的觀察者，也可以察覺到他的發現。

FOREWORD

Curiosity and conscience drive Wong How Man. Immersed in the tension between places as they were for many millennia and the stark change he sees emerging, How Man uses his photographer's eye to share his recognition of the impact of the incursion of the outside world. His journalistic probing uncovers nascent issues. We, as viewers and readers, revel in his ventures and adventures wondering if we could have the insight and strength to herd reindeer in Siberia or revive the Burmese cat as a pure line or be a watchman over the source of the Irrawaddy or the chronicler of the disappearance of the Batak. In recent travels, How Man has widened his search to man-made phenomena such as the luthiers of Italy to remind us that all change in not found in nature.

How Man never judges. He observes and learns. He teaches — hoping that he will infect the next generation with the desire to explore methodically and record the facts so that a wider audience, those of us who are armchair observers, may become aware.

HM 所做的事激發我自己對亞洲的興趣。他告訴我過去與現在發生的故事。他讓我了解巨大的改變正在亞洲各地進行，不只是在經濟上、政治上，社群、人們、自然也同時在改變。他鮮明的描述讓我發覺原來亞洲存在著這些景象。HM 的這些故事和紀錄將會隨著時間而顯得更加重要。

Betsy Z. Cohen

創辦人 / 董事長，*The Bancorp*
大都會歌劇院董事，亞洲協會董事
名譽董事，大都會博物館

My own interest in Asia has been stimulated by How Man's work. He tells me stories of what was and what is. Thus, he allows me to understand the great changes being experienced throughout Asia not only economically and politically but in the ways in which communities, people and nature change. The graphic nature of his descriptions brings to life parts of the Asian landscape I never knew existed. How Man is creating a compendium of stories and a record of impact which will serve us better and better as time moves on.

Betsy Z. Cohen

Founder/Chairman, The Bancorp
Trustee, Metropolitan Opera, Asia Society
Hon Trustee, Metropolitan Museum

作者序

在伊洛瓦底江的上游為這兩本書寫序似乎是很合適的。我們的營地在海拔 3900 公尺處，離河流真正的源頭只有幾公里。但是從這裡到源頭還需要再爬升海拔 1000 公尺，加上只能徒步行走，確實是一段艱難的路。

有一位中國的遙感探測專家，他依據衛星影像，指出伊洛瓦底江的源頭是一個高山源湖。事實上，我和團隊在四個月前已經到過那個湖，這趟我們再次回來是為了尋找注入那個湖的一條溪流。

我們的 NASA 衛星影像專家馬丁〈Martin Ruzek〉告訴我，一年之中有 6 個月的雪融時期可以看到另外一條長達 1.4 公里的溪流，而這條溪流會注入那個高山源湖。因此，若只有抵達到那個源湖對我們來說是不夠的。我們知道一定要再回來確認這條亞洲最偉大的河流之一的源頭。這趟旅程在自然一書的最後一章裡有所描述。

PREFACE

It seems appropriate that I am writing this preface at the upper reaches of the Irrawaddy River. Our basecamp, at an altitude of 3900 meters, is only a few short kilometers from the actual river source. But to reach it from here will require some serious hiking and a climb of another 1000 meters in elevation.

According to one of China's foremost remote sensing experts who defined river sources through satellite images, an alpine source lake is the geographic source of the Irrawaddy. My team and I reached the source lake only four months ago, but are now returning to explore a stream that feeds the lake.

Our own NASA satellite image expert Martin Ruzek revealed to me that, during six months of the year when the snow was melted, it would expose another stream, 1.4 kilometers in length, feeding the lake. Thus reaching the source lake is simply not good enough for us. We know we must return to verify the ultimate source of one of the most important rivers of Asia. That journey is described in the last chapter of the book on nature.

這樣的舉動無疑地彰顯了探險的精神，為了得到這個世界的真正知識，我們必需灌注更多的執著和努力，即使這個知識僅是個很微小的細節。在我們抵達依洛瓦底江源頭的那個月裡我同時也書寫了另一篇在紐約市中心的體驗。那是完全不一樣的世界，不一樣的高度，關於帝國大廈。而這也正好呈現了人類生命中多樣的眼界與經歷，而探險正是這些經歷與知識的邊沿。

這兩本書，一本關於自然，另一本聚焦文化，是我系列書的第 19 和第 20 本，記錄我在實地的工作狀況以及旅途上的回顧。每個篇章都是致力於探險的累積，不斷地向前追求新知中，也同時追述我們保育工作項目的後續。

這兩本書裡的故事除了發生在中國之外，還有關於其他鄰近國家的記述，我希望帶著讀者跟著我到另一塊陸地和海洋，一起去看看這些我曾經走訪過的地區。希望你會喜歡這些旅程，當我的探險夥伴，與我一同經歷我所經歷。

黃效文
CERS 創辦人 / 會長
日期　二零一七年十月二日

This type of effort epitomizes what exploration spirit is about, an obsession and dedication to even the smallest details in order to attain additional knowledge about our physical world. Another piece, written within a month before reaching the Irrawaddy source, is diabolically different, in the heart of New York City, and to a very different height, that of the Empire State Building. It represents the diversity of our human experience, as exploration is precisely about probing the edges of experience and knowledge.

These two volumes of books, one on nature, the other on culture, are the 19th and 20th in a series chronicling my work in the field as well as my reflections during those journeys. They are the culmination of our perseverance in exploration and constant pursuit of knowledge, and at times recount our follow-on conservation endeavors.

The stories in these two books cover more than China and her neighboring countries, bringing our readers to regions I have had the opportunity to visit on other continents and even oceans. I hope you enjoy these journeys as you travel by my side.

Wong How Man
Founder/President CERS
October 2, 2017

船
家
之
歌
的
暮
光

TWILIGHT OF A RAFTER'S SONG

Kalewa, Myanmar – August 20, 2016

船家之歌的暮光 《竹筏上的緬甸》續篇

有六個女兒的東偉（*Thaung Wai*）肯定是個努力工作的人，他白天最好還是忙著點工作。他最辛苦的工作，就是在欽敦江上駕竹筏。他從 12 到 30 歲不等的女兒都尚未出嫁，但他的妻子多欽瑪桑（*Daw Khin Mar San*）似乎一點也不擔心。其實，她和丈夫不駕竹筏時，長女就在他們位於蒙育瓦的家庭工廠跟她一起幹活，這家家庭工廠製造緬甸人使用了兩千年以上的東西——焚香。

母女一天各自可以賺到約 2500 到 3000 緬元（2.5 到 3 美元），那得看她們完成多少件焚香或線香而定。平常，她們各自可做出 15000 到 18000 件。亦即每天要用掉五六根大竹子。而我剛搭乘的這艘由他們夫妻所駕駛的竹筏，是由 5000 根竹竿綁在一起造成的。

船家通常會低報竹根數量來隱瞞他們竹筏的規模，以混淆水運管制站。沿江有太多這種管制站了，每一站都在

Kalewa, Myanmar – August 20, 2016

TWILIGHT OF A RAFTER'S SONG

Sequel to Myanmar On A Raft

With six daughters, Thaung Wai must be a hard-working man, and he had better be busy working during the day. Thus he takes on one of the hardest jobs, rafting bamboo down the Chindwin River. Aged 12 to 30, none of his daughters is married, but his wife Daw Khin Mar San doesn't seem worried. In fact, as she gets off the raft, her eldest daughter joins her at work in their home factory in Monywa, a factory that manufactures something used for perhaps 2000 years or more by practically all Burmese – incense.

Mother and daughter each make approximately 2500 Kyat to 3000 Kyat a day (USD2.5 to 3), depending on how many pieces of incense, or joss sticks, they finish. On an average day, they can make 15,000 or 18,000 pieces each. That would translate into the use of five or six large bamboo stems per day. And the raft I just boarded, operated by the husband and wife, is constructed of 5,000 bamboo stems bound together.

Rafters tend to disguise the size of their raft by stating a lower number of stems in order to confuse the marine control posts. There are too many such

勒索經過的貨船，而民間的船家根本沒有能力反抗。其實這些寄生蟲完全沒有能力算出竹子實際的數量，因為有些淹在水面下。五千根似乎是個合理的平均數。要是不幸遇上太多這些「水蛭」，船家奔波忙碌之餘還可能會賠錢甚至搞到破產。

竹子的旅程始於緬甸與印度邊界的深山中。只有那些長得巨大的叢林竹子才值得做成竹筏，然後沿著欽敦江漂流而下。伐竹工採收竹子後，沿著小溪把它送到北方大鎮霍馬林。東偉和老婆會在那裡以每根 450 緬元採購。然而若是在源頭處收購，每根可能只需要花 150 緬元。

收集並組裝一艘大竹筏大概要花一個月，竹子疊起來像個房子。而從霍馬林駕駛這種尺寸的竹筏漂流到蒙育瓦的下游販賣，至少要花上一個月。在雨季時工作尤其是辛苦。

Chindwin Bamboo raft / 欽敦江的竹筏

posts along the river, each imposing a levee on passing boats with cargo, especially private rafters with no channel for reprieve. These parasites would not be able to count the actual number of bamboos, some of which are submerged under water. And 5,000 seems a good even number. If unfortunately hit by too many of these water "leeches", a rafter may run a deficit and be bankrupted by the journey.

The journey for the bamboo started deep in the hills bordering Myanmar and India. Only jungle bamboo growing to huge sizes are worthy of raft-making and floating down the Chindwin. The cutters harvest the bamboo and bring them down along small streams until they get to Homalin, a sizable town in the north. From there Thaung and his wife would buy the bamboo at 450 Kyats each. Others who acquired the bamboo from its source may pay only 150 Kyats per piece.

Simple kitchen / 簡陋的廚房

Brewing tea / 煮茶

雖然水流變快，但是也比較危險，尤其在過彎處。在這種位置，裝在竹筏末端的小馬達能幫他們通過水流凶險的角落。時間對這種工作似乎不重要，因為水流決定了竹筏行進的速度。當然，竹筏在夜間也會靠岸。

三餐都在竹筏上烹煮，沿途收集到的漂流木成為所需的燃料。通常駕一艘竹筏需要三個人，所以常有親戚跟來幫忙。這種竹筏沒有船頭或船尾，因為水流可能突然把

Preparing raft c.1985 / 約 1985 年組裝竹筏的情景

It takes about a month to collect and assemble a large raft, one that has bamboo walls stacked up on the sides like a house. From Homalin, to float a raft of that size down to below Monywa where it is sold would take upward of a month. Rainy season makes the work particularly hard. Though the river flows faster, it is also more dangerous, especially when rounding a bend. At such locations, a small motor attached to one end of the raft helps them negotiate around the corner where the current can be treacherous. Time seems irrelevant in such a venture, as the flow of the river will determine the speed of the raft. Of course, the raft stays ashore during the night.

Meals are cooked onboard the raft, fuel being dried drift wood collected along the way. Usually it takes three persons to handle a raft, thus a relative would generally come along. There is no bow or stern to such a raft, as the current may spin it around and suddenly the former bow would become the stern. Thus a long rudder protrudes from each end of the raft to assist in steering the raft.

I recall in the mid-1980s while working on covering the Yangtze River in China, I encountered frequent bamboo rafters as well as log rafters in the mid-section of the river, both above and below Chongqing. Within a few short years, all rafters disappeared. They were replaced by more efficient road or boat transport, and were also considered a hazard for other river vessels. It seems the days of the rafters on the Chindwin are likewise numbered. It is important that we now document their last days before this too becomes part of history.

船頭變成船尾。所以竹筏兩端都有突出的長舵好控制方向。

我記得在八〇年代中期報導中國長江時，在中游的重慶附近經常看到竹筏跟木筏船家。短短幾年內，所有船家都消失了。被更有效率的公路或船運取代，他們甚至被其他船隻視為是危害。欽敦江上的船家似乎也同樣來日無多。我們現在很重要的工作是在這些也變成歷史之前，紀錄下他們的歲月。

遇到東偉的竹筏一週後，我們造訪了他們位於蒙育瓦下游兩小時船程外欽敦江岸邊的家。傾盆大雨中機車載我們抵達，進入 *Yay Sa Kyo* 鎮的瑞金村（*Shwe Kyaung*）。大多數民家圍牆外或庭院裡堆著大量的竹子。很顯然這個村子從事跟竹子有關的產業。

我們渾身濕透，在村裡的巷弄又在淹水後泥濘不堪，經過一番跋涉我們才找到了東偉的家。他老婆一聽說我們來訪，馬上衝出家門迎接。原來他們也才剛到家一會兒。我們在江上一天的移動距離，他們可是得要花上七天。我在豪雨中搭機車的 *15* 分鐘路程也只是稍微體驗一下他們一週的經歷，更何況他們還是在竹筏上。

A week after our rendezvous with Thaung Wai's raft, we visited their home some two hours boat distance below Monywa along the Chindwin. As the motorcycles took us to the home in pouring rain, we entered the village of Shwe Kyaung in the township of Yay Sa Kyo. Most homes have large stacks of bamboo lying outside their fence or inside their courtyard. It is obvious that this village is engaged with the business of bamboo.

Drenched from head to toe, we found Thaung Wai's house after tramping through some flooded muddy village alleys. When his wife Daw Khin Mar San learned of our visit, she rushed out of her house to greet us. It turned out they too had just arrived home a short moment ago. What took our boat a day to cover in river distance had taken them seven days to complete. The pouring rain of my 15-minute journey on a motorcycle was a tiny taste of what they had gone through during the last week, and more, on a raft.

After a round of tea, we observed how the daughters and a relative made both incense sticks as well as weaving of baskets. The baskets are sold from 1500 to 2000 kyats depending on sizes. One daughter told me that the yearly flood had just gone through their villages and had now subsided. It usually takes twenty days for the flood to recede. During the flood, water may be waist-high and everyone moved to the loft, living near the ceiling of the house. I noticed a neighbor's kitchen was set up on a small floating platform, sitting on four metal drums. At the moment of our visit, the drums were on rather wet

喝過茶之後，我們看著他的女兒們和親戚如何製作線香與編竹籃。根據大小，竹籃可以賣 1500 到 2000 緬元不等。其中一個女兒告訴我，年度例行的洪水才剛經過他們村子，現在水已經退了。通常要花上二十天的時間洪水才會退去。洪水來時可能會淹到腰部，所以大家都搬到距離天花板最近的閣樓上去住。我發現有位鄰居的廚房被放在漂浮的小平台上，平台底下是四個鐵桶。我們造訪時，鐵桶下方還相當潮溼。附近有位阿婆坐著喃喃自語，跟我們說她 140 歲了；旁人很快地提醒她其實只有 104 歲。

我們想買兩個剛從生產線出來，編得很漂亮的籃子。但是多欽瑪桑堅持要送給我們當禮物。他們擁有的雖少，卻非

Daughter working bamboo / 處理竹子的女兒

ground. Nearby, an old lady sat and mumbled to herself, telling us that she was 140 years old. Others soon reminded her that she was only 104.

We tried to buy two nicely knitted baskets, fresh off the production line. But Daw Khin Mar San insisted on offering those as her gifts. Little though they have, they are very generous. I urged one of the ladies to follow us back to our boat so I could dig up some goodies for the family. Fortunately I had six CERS bags to return the favor, one for each of her daughters.

As we sailed on, I knew the rafter's time-honored profession had entered into its twilight years. As Myanmar modernizes, a more efficient mode of travel coupled with greedy officials extorting unreasonable fees would soon spell the

Making incence sticks / 製作線香

常慷慨。我邀請一名女士跟我們一起回到船上，好讓我挖些好東西送給這家人。幸好我還有六個探險學會的袋子可以當作回禮，送給她的女兒們，剛好一人一個。

當我們繼續在河面上航行時，我知道這種歷史悠久的船家行業已經步入了夕陽期。隨著緬甸的現代化，更有效率的運輸方式加上貪婪官員的勒索，很快地就會讓古老的傳統消失。希望我們的影片能對欽敦江竹筏船伕的辛苦生活表達最後的致敬。

一根竹子
三千件焚香
五千根竹子的竹筏非常合理
千百年來深受寺廟喜愛
敬神食糧的這些東西
六支線香一緬元
母女可賺 6000 餘
哀悼筏人暮歌
明天回憶逝去

Shadow of rafter / 駕筏人的影子

demise of an ancient tradition. Our film would hopefully pay a last tribute to the hard life of the rafting boatman of the Chindwin River.

One bamboo, three thousands incense

Five thousand piece raft makes perfect sense

For centuries temples find it good

Such objects offer gods as food

One Kyat paid for six joss sticks

Mother and daughter 6000 Kyats would make

Today I mourn the rafter's twilight song

As tomorrow all but memories are by gone.

三十年前的中國

CHINA
30 YEARS AGO

San Francisco – September 13, 2016

三十年前的中國

我從 1974 年起就到中國，前後工作了四十多年，今年適逢 CERS 卅週年，用那個時代的照片來回顧一下特殊的 1986 年似乎很應景。

那年我開始為美國國家地理雜誌報導了長江下游，跟著是 CERS 第一次進入中國南方邊境的貴州與雲南省探險。

在侗族和苗族等少數民族的節慶月去探訪，確實讓我拍到了一些非常好的照片，並且也收集了不少民族學的藏品和服裝。之後在西雙版納探訪傣族與德宏景頗族，也為我們帶來了許多成果。

Yangtze alligator medicine vendor / 長江鱷魚藥小販

CHINA 30 YEARS AGO

Though I have worked in China since 1974 for over 40 years, this year marks CERS' 30th and it seems appropriate to revisit that special year 1986 with a gallery of photos from that era.

The year started off with my coverage of the lower Yangtze for the National Geographic, followed by the first CERS expedition to China's southern border provinces of Guizhou and Yunnan.

Returning to visit the Dong and Miao minorities during a festive month yielded some superb pictures, as well as ethnographic objects and costumes to enrich our growing photo archive and artifact collection. The visit to the Dai

Goose run / 運送鵝

應西藏總書記楊候第先生之邀飛到拉薩，獲准進入拍
攝布達拉宮內部，包括內殿，達賴喇嘛的住所與寢室，
這是不對外開放的區域，即使宮內的人也很難得看見。

這些動人的影像對一個年輕活躍的組織是個光明的序
曲，這組織就是香港中國探險學會，現在簡稱 CERS。

people of Xishuangbanna and the Dehong Jingpo people followed with additional results.

I flew to Lhasa as guest of Tibet Secretary General Mr Yang Haudi. I was allowed to photograph inside the Potala Palace, including the inner sanctum of the Dalai Lama's residence and bed room, an area not open to the public, and rarely seen even by insiders.

These illustrious images seem a very promising overture of what were to come later for a young and vibrant organization, the China Exploration & Research Society, now known as CERS.

Ge ethnic group / 仡佬族

Kachin /Jingp nationality / 克欽族 / 景頗族
De-An nationality / 德安族

Dai nationality / 傣族
Dong nationality / 侗族

Miao nationality / 苗族
Dalai Lama's bedroom in the Potala / 達賴喇嘛在布達拉宮的臥室

再訪那伽獵頭族領域

RETURN TO NAGA HEAD HUNYER'S TERRITORY

Lahe, Khamti of Myanmar – January 16, 2017

再訪那伽獵頭族領域

我經常搭乘空中巴士客機。至於空中卡車，只有兩次——第一次是四年前，再來就是現在。我一點也不期待，若不是這台空中卡車會帶我到印緬邊界去參加一年一度的那伽族慶典。這些空中卡車比 *Nike* 打著麥可・喬丹名號推出的喬丹鞋更酷，肯定也更彈跳。稱作空中卡車是因為乘客要坐在車頂，享受天上的涼風。像這次遇上那伽族山上的冬天，則是寒風。至於彈跳，雖說有點輕描淡寫，但實在是找不到更好的字眼了。

我戴上帽子、圍巾和面紗以阻擋陽光及風沙，活像個叛亂軍或恐怖份子。這些山上真的有叛亂軍，延伸越界到印度那邊不時有動亂的那伽族領域。但是在緬甸這邊，狀況緩和多了。已經看不到四年前的哨兵大隊，至少不像以前那麼明目張膽出現。

CERS 四人小隊是去年才成為觀光旅遊部部長翁孟（*U Ohn Maung*）的客人。若不是受邀的話我們就得付一大筆錢給旅行社，因為這家旅行社壟斷了這項年度活動。

RETURN TO NAGA HEAD HUNTER'S TERRITORY

I have flown a lot on Airbus. As for AirTruck, only twice – the first time was four years ago and now again. It is something I wasn't quite looking forward to, except the destination where this truck is taking me, to the once-a-year Naga Festival along the Myanmar border with India. These AirTrucks are more cool and definitely more bouncy than Air Jordans, the Nike shoes bearing Michael Jordan's name. It is called AirTruck because the passengers sit on top, enjoying the cool air from above. And in this case in the winter of the Naga hills, it's cold air. As for bouncy, it is an understatement for lack of a better word.

Covering myself with a hat, neck cloth and face-veil to shield the sun and the dust, I resembled some kind of an insurgent or terrorist. Insurgents there are indeed in these hills, extending into the at-times turbulent territories of Naga-land on the Indian side of the border. On the Myanmar side however, things have settled down quite a bit. The many military sentries four years ago are no longer in sight, or at least not as blatantly visible as before.

My small CERS team of four is guests of my long-time friend U Ohn Maung

相對地作為回禮，我們要幫旅遊部製作一支廣告片，推廣那伽族山區部落這個多采多姿的慶典，直到不久前他們還是以獵人頭聞名呢。

這五個小時的車程裡，大部分的時候這部四驅車都打在低檔，上上下下翻越許多很陡的斜坡。不像四年前全程都是泥土路，今年最難走的路段還有「柏油路」，可以產生更多的摩擦力。連那間我們住過設在餐廳樓上可以俯瞰勒黑鎮最大的十字路口的臨時民宿，都升級了。

現在不必再睡地上的草蓆，終於有床了，只是會軋軋作響的床其實是向民家借來的。牆上掛著 2014 年印著全彩照片的免費月曆，由那伽人民共和國印製。彩色照片描繪印度那伽族的軍隊和獨立運動的領袖。

新的文人政府上台後，軍人隱身在後，但同時必定會擴充警力。曾經士兵手上常見的自動機關槍變得罕見。也許緬甸真的變了。一月十三日，那伽族部落開始前來，一村接著一村。我們利用這天探訪附近三個村子。「附近」的意思是在崎嶇地形上開車至少一小時以外的地方。

who became Minister of Hotels & Tourism last year. Otherwise we would have to pay a rather exorbitant price to the one travel agency which, as the only tour operator, monopolizes this annual event. In return, we will produce a trailer film for the ministry to promote this colorful festival of the Naga hill tribe, until quite recently best known for their head hunting practice.

The five-hour ride, much of which on low-gear four-wheel drive, negotiated up and down many slopes with extreme gradient. Unlike four years ago when the entire route was dirt and mud, this year the most difficult parts have been "paved", allowing for better traction. Even the temporary "hostel" where we stayed above a restaurant overlooking the biggest crossroad of Lahe town, has been upgraded.

Rather than sleeping on the floor with a straw mat, there are beds now, though squeaky - they came borrowed from some homes. On the wall hung a complimentary calendar with full-color photos from 2014, printed by the People's Republic of Nagaland. Full-color photos depict the army forces and leaders of independence movement of the Naga on the Indian side of the border.

With the new civilian government in place, army presence was kept to a minimum, whereas police force must have been expanded. The once-prevalent automatic machine guns carried by soldiers can hardly be seen. Perhaps Myanmar has really turned a corner. On January 13, Naga tribes began to

Warriors ritual dance / 戰士舞

再訪那伽獵頭族領域

arrive, village by village. We took the day to visit three nearby villages. Nearby easily means an hour or so of tough-terrain driving.

Things remained much the same as four years ago and these villages still look primitive and dilapidated. Modern changes to Myanmar cities like Yangon and Mandalay are not reflected here at all, perhaps with the exception of young men with mobile phones. There are obviously no mobile services reaching far out to such locales. But that does not stop young folks from using the device as a camera to share photos and music of choice.

All that backwardness however may be about to change, with the arrival by Army helicopter of two loads of advance party to the festival ground. This was followed by a white helicopter with the Myanmar tri-color flag on it. The President of Myanmar was making a special appearance at the festival. He stayed for two full days throughout the festival, including meetings with local leaders. To come this far despite his busy schedule is a major commitment

情況跟四年前差不多，這些村子看起來仍然原始破舊。仰光與曼德勒等緬甸城市的現代化完全沒輻射到這裡，除了年輕人手上拿著手機以外。這麼偏遠的地方顯然沒有手機訊號，但這並沒有阻止年輕人將手機當成相機去分享他們喜歡的照片和音樂。

然而這落後的景象即將改變，軍方直升機載來兩批先遣部隊到慶典場地。接著一架印著緬甸三色旗的白色直升機也來了。緬甸總統特別蒞臨這個慶典。整整兩天的活動他都在，他也撥空接見了地方領袖。能在百忙之中抽空到這個偏遠地區參加慶典，可能透露了他會與這偏鄉約十二萬的那伽族和平相處。

慶典正熱鬧的時候我們參加了官方的午宴終於有機會與總統見面，並短暫地聊了一下。他很驚訝我就是那個將

of time, perhaps reflecting on the importance he would accord this distant land with only 120,000 or so Naga people.

Over an official lunch during the height of the festival, we had the chance to meet and chat briefly. He was surprised that I was instrumental in reintroducing the Burmese Cats to Myanmar. Just two months ago, he visited our Burmese Cat Sanctuary at Inle Lake. He told me that he held his favorite cat for over half an hour during the visit, and said he was a cat lover. I asked if he would like to have a Burmese and he replied that unless he could care for the cat himself, he would prefer not to have one at this time. But he could wait.

The festival was attended by 31 foreign guests four years ago and this year we had 48 in total, still a relatively small number considering this is the only time in the entire year that the place is open to outside visitors and then but for three days. I counted two dozen at most, as the others were special guests from Yangon or Mandalay.

While the festival is organized by the government to demonstrate solidarity, the Naga tribes from far-out villages had to walk for long distance to attend, some for up to two days. This year there are fewer tribes than four years ago and the number from each tribe seems to have diminished. Some new activities had been added besides the more spectacular ritual dances and chanting. Sports events like volley ball, rattan caneball, tug-of-war, to even a 21Km

HM met President at lunch / 午宴時 HM 與總統會面
President with Naga hat / 總統戴著那伽族帽子

緬甸貓重新帶回緬甸的人。就在兩個月前，他拜訪過我們在茵萊湖的緬甸貓園。他告訴我他在那裡抱著他最喜愛的一隻貓半個多小時，說他也是愛貓人。我問他是否也想要一隻緬甸貓時，他回答除非他能親自照顧，否則這時候寧可不養。但是他可以等。

四年前的這個慶典有 31 位外賓參加，而今年總共有 48 位，鑒於這是這個區域整年唯一對外國訪客開放的三天，人數仍然算少。在我看來頂多只有廿幾位外國訪客，因為其餘的都是從仰光或曼德勒來的。

慶典雖由政府主辦以展現團結，但是位在偏遠的那伽族部落必須長途跋涉才能參加，有些還要走上兩天。今年前來的部落比四年前少，而且人數也少了。除了這些比較有看頭的傳統舞蹈和歌唱表演外，也新增了一些活動。像是排球、藤球、拔河比賽，甚至還有一個 21 公里的馬拉松，在山丘間的泥土路上上下下。

馬拉松在早晨六點天還沒亮的時候就起跑。日出後不久，冠軍就衝過終點線。他的紀錄是一小時四十三分。亞軍和季軍不久也陸續出現，大概只間隔五分鐘左右。兩人都穿著帆布鞋，但是輸給穿拖鞋賽跑的冠軍。每位贏家各得到一支高露潔牙膏，冠軍得到微薄的一萬

marathon through a hill circuit of up and down dirt tracks.

The marathon began at 6am in darkness. Soon after sunrise, the champion ran pass the finish line. His time was one hour forty-three minutes. The First and Second Runners-up soon turned up, perhaps five minutes or so apart. Both of them had canvas shoes on, yet losing to the Champion who ran on flip-flops. Each winner was given a tube of Colgate toothpaste, and the Champion had a small cash prize of 10,000 Kyats, equivalent to about US Eight Dollar. While the organizer claimed that 59 runners participated, we saw few passing the finish line. Perhaps some may simply ran home.

As in previous year, the official announcement by the emcee was done strictly in Burmese language followed by brief English translation. Few if any of the Naga tribes attending would understand even Burmese. Only sign of support and integration was the President wearing a Naga hat and vest. It would be more proper if in future Naga language could also be used for the event.

Furthermore, the pop music by a live band on stage obliterated the tradition-al wild chants of the Naga warriors. No wonder only two groups cared to play on their traditional long drum, relegated to an obscure corner of the fair ground. In the past, almost all groups spent time in unison beating of the drum, something unique to Naga culture and related to battle calls and return of a triumphant head-hunting expedition. Such an eclipse of the Naga culture

緬元獎金，大約是八美元。主辦單位宣稱 59 位跑者參
加，但我們發現沒有多少人通過終點線。或許有些人就
直接跑回家了。

跟往年一樣，司儀只有使用緬語加上簡短的英語翻譯。
前來參加的那伽族人沒幾個聽得懂緬甸語。唯一能展
現出支持族群融合的動作就是總統身上穿戴著那伽族
的帽子和背心。如果未來的慶典中也能夠使用那伽族
語，那麼應該會比較恰當吧。

此外，舞台上樂團表演的流行音樂完全抹殺了那伽族戰
士傳統狂野的歌聲。難怪只有兩個團體願意用傳統的長
鼓演奏，其餘時間它就被丟在角落。在過去，大夥兒會
聚在一起打鼓，這個對那伽族文化有獨特意義；出征作
戰打鼓，成功地獵人頭後凱旋歸來也打鼓。那伽族文化
的消逝令人傷心。在仰光保存殖民風格的偽緬甸建築得
到許多關注，但是同時正在消失的原住民文化卻幾乎沒
人在意或願意保存它，這讓我覺得很奇怪。

好幾家緬甸電視台前來記錄這場慶典，但是聚焦多落在
總統的一舉一動。他們不只在地面拍攝，還有至少四架
無人機不時在我們頭上打轉。它們吸引那伽族人不停地
抬頭往天空看，相當干擾慶典與演出。

was disheartening. It seems strange to me that preserving pseudo-Burmese architecture with colonial overtone got so much attention in Yangon whereas the disappearing of living indigenous culture receive little notice or support.

Several Myanmar television channels were on hand to record the festival, more so focusing on the President's every movement. Not only were they filming on the ground, there were at least four drones at different times above us. This turned out to be a major distraction throughout the ceremonies and performances, with the Naga heads all turning to the sky.

Naga beating long-drum / 那伽族打長鼓

在表演與歡慶活動的空檔之餘，我們收集到一小批那伽族文物。包括野豬獠牙和犀鳥羽毛做的戰士帽、一把那伽族劍、雕刻著一個人手拿兩支長矛的竹製酒筒、有圖案和動物頭骨裝飾的項鍊以及各種手工織布做成的毯子和布料。有些文物品是花了漫長的交涉和唇舌才弄到手。但最寶貴的文物是一件用花冠皺盔犀鳥首所裝飾的手織籃子。整批收藏很快地會擺在我們 *HM Explorer* 號的上層甲板展示，搭配一個收藏緬甸相關書籍的圖書櫃。

慶典結束後，空中卡車的喇叭響起，催促我們上車回到欽敦江邊的坎迪鎮，從那裡我們飛回曼德勒。不停地走訪村落又睡在硬床上，使得我全身有點痠痛。才四天沒洗澡，沒刮鬍子，鬍鬚已經長的濃密。我很不情願地在深夜四點半掙扎起床，因為卡車要在五點天還沒亮的黑暗中出發。無疑四天前顛簸路途的記憶仍很鮮明，猶在目前。

In between all the performances and festivities, we managed to collect a small number of Naga artefacts. Among them is a warrior hat with boar tusks and a Hornbill feather, a Naga sword, a bamboo liquor container with stylized motif of a person with two spears, various hand-woven textiles in the form of blankets or plaited cloth, and necklaces with images and animal skulls. Some pieces were acquired after long rounds of negotiation and persuasion. But the most prized piece is a hand-woven basket decorated with the head of a Wreathed Hornbill. The entire collection would soon be put on display on the upper deck of the HM Explorer, our research vessel, complementing a special library of books on Myanmar.

As the festival came to a close, the AirTruck horn was blowing, urging us to again ride back to Khamti town by the Chindwin River, from where we would fly back to Mandalay. My body was aching a bit from the hike to villages as well as from the hard bed I slept on. I had not had a bath for only four days and my beard was growing thicker. I pushed myself out of bed at 4:30 as the truck was to leave at 5am in darkness. But my butt was dragging. No doubt its memory was still fresh with apprehension from the bouncy ride of just four days ago.

Naga hats with hornbill feather / 用犀鳥羽毛裝飾的那伽族帽子

貴州的懸棺

HANGING COFFINS OF GUIZHOU

Getu River, Guizhou – February 14, 2017

貴州的懸棺

「抬頭看看，這裡有些懸棺。」船老大頭也不回稀鬆平常地對著一群十來個跟我們同搭一艘小汽艇的觀光客說。遊客們來此遊河，船隻沿著格凸河最美麗的地方行進，峽谷兩側有高聳石灰岩山。

我們的小隊主要是前來調查懸棺的。但是懸棺所在的位置很危險，船家不肯為我們停船。每個人都要去附近的苗族村莊。大多數的人兩小時內就會搭上回程船。至於我們，我們打算留在村裡繼續我們的研究。

駐香港的 CNN 記者凱蒂・杭特最近給我看了幾張貴州西南部山洞裡的懸棺照片。我很想馬上去看看。從 30 年前 CERS 成立以來我們一直在研究這個題目。我跟隊員們去過許多地方的懸棺遺跡，也包括保存一個最古老最不為人所知的懸棺遺址。

我從未聽說過貴州省內也有懸棺遺址。所以這個新資訊令我非常興奮。我調整我的行程趕在農曆年過後兩

HANGING COFFINS OF GUIZHOU

"Look up above your head, here are a few of the hanging coffins," said the boat driver casually without turning his head, addressing a dozen or so tourists who were sharing the same motor launch as us. Visitors come here for the 20-minute boat ride along a most beautiful stretch of the Getu River with limestone hills rising on both sides of the gorge.

My small team came mainly to inspect the coffins. But at this precarious location where the coffins were suspended in mid-air, the boat would not stop for us. Everyone was on way to a nearby Miao village. Most would take the return trip within a couple hours. Whereas for us, we intend to stay in the village to pursue our own agenda.

Katie Hunt, a CNN journalist based in Hong Kong, recently showed me a few images of coffins inside a cave from southwestern Guizhou. I wanted to go at once to have a look. This topic has been one of our ongoing studies since CERS's inception 30 years ago. My team and I had made many visits to various hanging coffin sites, including preserving one of the least known and oldest hanging coffin locations.

Getu River drains into cave / 格凸河流進山洞

週抵達格凸河，它位在苗族與布依族少數民族自治區
的紫雲縣南方。

這個村子叫做 *Gebuncun* 格丼村，但現在又稱大河苗寨，
或大河苗村。「丼」是個罕見字，所以幾乎沒人知道怎麼
發音。字看起來很簡單，井字裡面加一個點。我聽說，
很具象地，字的發音就像石頭丟進井裡的回音，咚。

河的名字格凸也具圖象意義。河在這裡被兩座巨大險峻

I had never heard of such burial sites within Guizhou Province. So this new information got me excited. I adjusted my calendar and left for Guizhou two weeks after Chinese New Year. We arrived at Getu River south of the county town of Ziyun, an area inhabited by the Miao and Buyi minorities.

The village was called Gebuncun, but now simply known as Da He Miao Jai or Big River Miao Village. "Bun" is a character rarely seen, thus hardly anyone knew how to pronounce the word. It looks rather simple, a dot inside the word for a water well. I was told, most graphically, that it is pronounced exactly like the sound and echo produced when a stone is dropped into a well, bung.

Getu, the name of the river, is likewise graphic. The river here is cut off on both ends by two huge and precipitous limestone hills, each with a gigantic cave rising close to a hundred meters above the water. The river comes from inside one cave and, on the other end, enters into the other cave; thus the word Ge, meaning divided. Tu means 'protruding' or 'special', referring to the river appearing in between the two hills.

For me what is Tu, or so special about this place, was the hanging coffins. We stayed at a modest and clean traditional Miao lodging house. Wang Xiao-er, meaning Wang Number Two, is the Miao owner. Hu Yixiang, his most jolly wife and a Buyi nationality from a nearby village, was home to greet us and

的石灰岩山切斷，每座山都有離水面將近一百米的大山洞。河流來自一個山洞，在另一端，進入另一個山洞；所以用格字，表示區分。凸表示「凸出」或「突出」，指的是河出現在兩座山之間。

在我看來，這裡最突出最特別的就是懸棺。我們住在一棟簡樸乾淨的傳統苗族民宿。苗族老闆叫做王小二。他開朗的老婆胡亦香〈音譯〉是來自鄰村的布依族，她在家迎接我們，也是我們的廚師。我問了她要怎麼樣才能去看剛才遊船那些在峽谷高處的懸棺。

「那些是一年多前才放上去的，」她給了令人意外的答案。「週末假日時太多觀光客來，小河擠滿了船隻。經營這個風景區的公司認為讓觀光船最遠只能到我們村子，然後在這裡折返是比較有效率的，」胡女士說。

Da He Miao Jai village / 大河苗寨村

acted as our cook. I asked her about visiting the coffins I had just seen high above us inside the gorge as we sailed through.

"Those were put up there just over a year ago," came her surprising answer. "Too many tourists are coming on weekends and holidays and the small river is cluttered with limited boats available. The company operating this tourist site find it more efficient to only allow tourist boats to come as far as our village, before turning back," added Hu.

"The real coffin site is further up, another 15 minutes or more to where the river came out of the cave. But to satisfy these tourists' curiosity about the coffins, a great selling point for the visit, the operator decided to fabricate some new ones along the way," Hu explained. The plot seems to have worked as these new coffins certainly look quite real and dramatic from afar, and should satiate the appetite of any normal tourist.

Wang with wife Hu and son / 老王、妻子和兒子 · Overhead coffins / 懸棺

「真正的懸棺遺址在更上游，從河流出山洞處再走 15 分鐘左右。但為了滿足觀光客對懸棺的好奇，是這裡的一大賣點，公司決定沿路放一些假的。」她解釋。計策似乎很成功，因為這些假懸棺看起來相當逼真也很戲劇性，應該能滿足一般遊客的胃口。

我就不同了。我執意要看這些升天的，真的懸棺。於是迅速擬定計畫，隔天早上由一位當地苗族人用他自己的船帶我們溯河到真正的遺址。時候不早了，我們吃完她為我們準備的美味晚餐後就回去休息。但是那晚卻很吵，鄰居在家大肆宴客，喝酒又打牌。

隔天早上，吃過簡單早餐之後，我們就上路。40 歲的吳曉明是我們的船老大兼嚮導。他來自上游不遠處另一個苗族村落榕榮村。現在，觀光客都在下游的村子折返，要到上游只能靠當地船隻開到一座漂浮竹橋為止。從這裡我們換乘更小的船繼續行程。

雖然風景很美麗，但我只急著去上游兩公里外的懸棺遺址。沒想到繞過一個轉彎，一座大山洞就出現在我們面前，山洞矗立在幾百公尺高、壯麗的石灰岩懸崖下，景觀令人屏息。格凸河消失到洞穴裡，有塊巨岩像一道門

Not so for me. I am hell-bent on seeing the heaven-bound bodies in the real coffins. A plan was soon made for a local Miao man to take us upriver to the real site with his private boat the next morning. In the meantime, it was getting late and we retired after a wonderful meal cooked by Hu. That evening a rather loud and huge banquet with sumptuous meal, drinking and card games was underway at our neighbor's house.

The following morning, after a brisk breakfast, we were on our way. Wu Xiaoming, 40 years old, was our boat driver/guide. He came from Rongle, another Miao village a short distance up the river. These days, tourists turn back at the lower village and the upper reaches can only be reached by local boats that travel up to a floating bamboo bridge. From here we changed to an even smaller boat to continue with our journey.

Despite the scenery being most beautiful, I was eager to get to the coffins site, which was only another two kilometres further upriver. As we rounded a corner, a huge cave under a majestic limestone cliff rising hundreds of meters was right in front of us. The spectacle was awe inspiring. The Getu river disappeared inside the cave where a huge rock blocked its channel like a gate.

We docked our boat by a makeshift platform. High above us, perhaps thirty to fifty meters higher, were layers and stacks of wooden coffins. They rested at

將它擋下。

我們在一個臨時搭建的平台邊停船。頭頂上，大約三十
到五十米高處，堆疊著幾層木棺。它們被放在巨大山洞
裡的不同位置，棺材有一部分凸出懸在空中。不像我們
研究過的其他懸棺遺址，這裡的棺材被放在堅固的岩石
上，相當牢固。

我往上爬，目標對準位置最低的懸棺，有時候必須手
腳同時著地，匍匐著身體向上攀爬。很快就來到了懸
棺邊。這些棺木有些還很完整，有些相當老舊而且開
始解體。透過木板的破洞，我看得見棺木內部，看到
骨頭和一些腐朽的衣物。其中一具棺木，甚至有顆完
整的頭骨外露。也有紙錢，是最近到此的訪客供奉的。

我繼續爬，很快地來到高處一個大洞的入口，這裡以
前大概有十幾具棺木。棺板碎片散落在地面，到處都
有骨頭與小瓷器的碎片。老吳向我們透露以前的棺材
更多，可能有幾百具。但他說一次村民引發的火災意
外，毀掉了大多數。

老吳告訴我，他們祖先如何只把這些棺材當作臨時的安
息地，等待有朝一日可以遷回位於東方故鄉的故事。這

Stacks of coffins / 堆疊的棺材

various locations in this huge cave, with a section of the coffins jutting out into mid-air. Unlike other coffin sites we studied with coffins suspended in mid-air, here the coffins were quite securely anchored, resting on solid rock.

Climbing up, at times on my hands and knees as if prostrating upward, I aimed for the lowest coffin site. Soon I was right up next to the coffins. While some were still intact, many were quite old and falling apart. Through broken sections of the wooden boards, I could peek inside the coffins, seeing bones and some disintegrating clothing. At one coffin, even a full skull was exposed to view. There were also paper money showing, offer-

些傳說有多少真實仍待查證。

「在我小時候，大概十到十二歲，有些考古學家來這裡研究這些棺材。我記得他們算過有三百八十幾個。火災後到現在頂多只剩三十個。」老吳又說。他進一步推測有些棺材可能整副被偷，因為盜墓賊可能認為裡面有貴重文物。

看完整個山洞混亂的狀態，我認為這個遺址並沒有做過有組織性的研究或保護。逗留一小時之後，回到船上，往村子裡去。在中午抵達大河苗寨，剛好聽到煙火發射升空，某個重大的慶祝活動正在進行。

從遠近不同的村子裡來了很多苗族人，他們聚集在鄰居家的庭院裡，就是昨晚大開宴會直到深夜的地方。這些男人以十到十二人一組，圍著火鍋坐在地上吃飯。在露天廚房幫忙的婦女則是站著吃。其中兩桌，有人在吹著嗩吶，一種類似雙簧管的高音管樂器，配合小鼓的節奏。即興演奏的管弦樂隊輪流演奏著音樂。

我到處探聽，突然看到在宴會邊緣豎了個石墳還點著蠟燭，有焚香和米酒供品。追問之下，原來大家是在「慶祝」一位村中婦人的喪禮。最特別的是，這場邀集了

ings from recent visitors to the site.

I climbed further and was soon at the elevated entrance to a huge cave. There were maybe a dozen coffins at this last spot. Scattered on the ground around were broken pieces of coffin boards, and here and there were bones and small ceramic pieces. Wu revealed to us that there used to be many more coffins, perhaps hundreds. But he said an accidental fire by villagers destroyed most of them.

Old folks told stories of how their ancestors used these coffins as temporary resting place such that they could one day be moved back to their historical home further east in China. How true such legends are remains to be verified.

"When I was still a kid, maybe ten or twelve years old, some archaeologists came here to study these coffins. I remember they numbered the coffins to over 380 sets. Today at most only thirty remain after the fire," Wu recounted. He further speculated that some coffins might have been stolen entirely because grave thieves may believe there are valuable relics inside.

Seeing the entire place left in disarray and a mess, I believe no organized study or protection has been accorded to this burial site. After lingering for an hour, I descended to the river and we started our journey back to the village. We reached Da He Miao Za at noon, just in time to hear fireworks being set off

親戚和村民的盛宴竟然遲來了 15 年。15 年前婦人過世時，一子一女匆忙埋葬他們的母親，然後出外工作，一直等到存夠了錢後才終於回家來舉辦正式的喪禮。

過程中，有十幾個婦人列隊走到墓前放下她們的花束。她們跪下哭了起來。我看得出大概只有兩位是哭真的，其餘只是用手帕掩面假哭而已。

我被邀去一起吃飯，但是婉拒了，因為我覺得有點突兀。突然，我發現這個遲來的喪禮正是附近懸棺的最好比喻：只是暫厝，可能放好幾代或幾百年，等待一天終會回到他們祖先的故鄉。

Funeral celebration / 葬禮慶祝

into the air. A major celebration of some sort was just underway.

A lot of Miao people were around, coming from nearby and distant villages. They were all gathering in the yard of our neighbor's home, the same place where the evening before there was a big party late into the night. Group of ten or twelve of these men would sit around a low hotpot having a meal. Women who were helping in the open air kitchen would eat standing up. At two of these hotpot groups, some of the men were playing the Suola, a kind of high-pitched wind instrument like an oboe, to the beat of a small drum. These impromptu orchestras would take turn playing the music.

I nosed around and suddenly saw that at the edge of the party stood a stone grave with lit candles, incense and offering of rice wine. On further inquiry, it turned out that this is the funeral "celebration" of a deceased woman in the village. What is so extraordinary is that this big banquet for relatives and vil-

Land ownership deed offering / 地契   Women weeping at grave / 墳邊哭泣的婦女

Village elder of the Miao / 苗族長者

lagers was 15 years overdue. The one son and one daughter buried their mother summarily upon her death, then went away to work and save up enough money before finally returning home to host a proper funeral.

At one point, a line of a dozen or so women walked up to the grave and set down their flower bouquets. They knelt down at the grave to begin crying. I could tell that perhaps only two of the ladies were crying for real, while the others simply covered their faces with handkerchiefs in a mock cry to eulogize the deceased.

I was asked to join in the meal, but politely declined, as I felt a bit out of place. Suddenly, I realized that perhaps having a long-delayed funeral may be just an allegory for the hanging coffins nearby, as these coffins lay in peace for the moment, perhaps for generations or centuries, before they would one day be returned to their ancestral home.

遵義會議的福與禍

BLESSING AND CURSE OF THE ZUNYI MEETING

Zunyi, Guizhou – February 15, 2017

遵義會議的福與禍

萬籟俱寂，我聽見巷子對面傳來的耳語，聲音從圍繞這座古老建築的外牆之外傳來，或者更精確地說是從一棟用灰磚蓋的老舊建築後傳來。我住在新完工的凡人旅館 8201 號房，凡人意指「普通人的旅館」。我的窗外是個有圍牆和大庭院的建築物。

但是我這個凡人聽見的雜音是來自八十幾年前，1935年一月。聲音逐漸變大，這時我聽到有人在爭吵，還有有人拍桌子。我聽不太懂對話的內容，因為有很多南腔北調的中國方言，甚至夾雜幾句外語。應該是俄語，但也有幾句德語。

時間是寒冷的一月十五日，每個人都穿著厚重的衣服。這場會議或辯論持續了三天，精確地說，是三個晚上。為了保密，才十六歲的中國共產黨中央委員會的會議，選在晚上召開。過了午夜，持續到天亮，然後全部 20 個人各自回房間休息，準備隔天晚上繼續開會。

BLESSING AND CURSE OF THE ZUNYI MEETING

When all was quiet, I could hear the whisper from across the alley, behind the walls that encircled this ancient building, or more accurately an ensemble of old and grey brick buildings. I was staying in Room 8201, at the newly finished Fan Ren Hotel, or "Common People Hotel". Across my window is a walled compound with a huge courtyard.

But the noise this common person overhearing was from over 80 years ago, in January of 1935. It gradually escalated and by now I could hear it ensued to become some kind of an argument, punctuated by someone pounding on what may be a table. The conversations were almost unintelligible, as there were many different heavily accented dialects of Chinese, even a few words in between were uttered in a foreign language. It must be Russian, but with a few words in German.

It was on the 15th of a cold January and everyone was bundled in heavy clothes and coats. This meeting, or debate, lasted for three days. To be exact, three nights, as every night for secrecy, the meeting of the Central Committee of the young Communist Party of China, then barely a 16 years adolescent

這個年輕男孩組成的團隊正在逃亡中，他們是屬於叛軍團體的一部分。在遵義只是暫時停留，以便他們重新集結走散的軍隊，繼續前進，閃躲追兵的殺戮，亦即閃避來自蔣介石的國民黨的優勢兵力。這些年輕人剛輸了一場大戰元氣大傷，這已經是第五次交戰了。先前的戰鬥中，他們勉強還算能夠毫髮無傷地逃走。但最後這場仗可是個大災難。

這段行軍日後被稱作共產黨紅軍的史詩級長征，是件締造歷史的大事件。但在遵義，只是長征的開端。遵義之前，紅軍是由三個核心領袖指揮，博古（本名秦邦憲）、李德（奧托・布朗）和周恩來。

當時所謂的三人小組被要求檢討他們敗戰的原因。博古是當時黨的總書記，李德則是以莫斯科為中心的共產國際部（Comintern）派來的軍事顧問，這兩個人為失敗找了許多藉口。周恩來反而一肩挑起指責，自我檢討他們的錯估敵軍和戰術。

參與 1935 年這場會議的人，在 1949 年後大多都成為中國的領袖包括毛澤東，朱德，劉少奇，張聞天，王稼祥，林彪，陳雲，彭德懷，楊尚昆，還有幾位紅軍的核心指揮官。鄧小平雖然當時在場但並沒被記載，直到 1984

boy, started in the evening. It would go pass midnight, lasted through the morning before everyone, 20 of them all, retired to each of their quarters, getting ready for meeting again the next evening.

This boys' club, all part of an insurgent group of soldiers, were on the run. The stop at Zunyi was just temporary, such that they could re-gather their dispersing forces, and continued on an evasive move, from the onslaught of a pursuing army, that of Chiang Kai-shek's Kuomintang far superior forces. The boys had just lost a major battle with devastating damage to their strength, the fifth in a series of punishing battles. In the earlier battles, they managed to escape relatively unscathed. But this last battle had been a disaster.

Door to Zunyi Meeting / 通往遵義會議的門

年才證實他當時也參與了那個會議。但在當時，楊尚昆和鄧小平身為資淺黨員，沒有參與激烈的辯論太多。這些領袖有許多人後來在延安的紅軍基地被排擠，或在文化大革命中被剷除。

當時說好會議只用來檢討軍事錯誤以決定紅軍接下來的行動，不會討論政治議題。不料張聞天率先扣扳機大力抨擊三人小組的錯誤，毛澤東則對當下軍情做了仔細的分析。毛進一步定義他的非傳統閃躲式游擊策略，用來反制裝備與數量佔絕對優勢的敵人。

The continuation of this forced march would later become known as the epic Long March of the Communist Red Army, a history-making event. But while at Zunyi, the Long March was only at its infancy. Prior to Zunyi, the Red Army was commanded by a core leadership of three men, Bo Gu (real name Qin Bangxian), Li De (Otto Braun) and Zhou En-lai.

The Three-person Group, as it was then known, were asked to review the reason of their defeat. The former two, Bo Gu was the General Secretary of the Party at the time, with Li De being the military advisor dispatched by the Comintern (Communist International) then centered in Moscow, provided numerous excuses for their loss. Zhou, in turn, took the blame squarely on his shoulder and made a self-criticism of their wrong assessment of the strength and tactics of the enemy.

At this meeting in 1935, almost all of China's future leaders after 1949 were present, Mao Tse-tung, Zhu De, Liu Shaoqi, Zhang Wentian, Wang Jiaxiang, Lin Biao, Chen Yun, Peng Dehuai, Yang Shangkun, as well as several core commanders of the Red Army. Deng Xiaoping, though present, was not accounted for until much later in 1984 when he verified that he was a participant at the meeting. But at the time, both Yang Xangkun and Deng must be junior members and did not participated much in the heated debate. Many of these leaders were later side-lined at the Red Base of Yenan, or purged during the Cultural Revolution.

新的三人軍事領導小組於此建立，接下來八年張聞天擔任總書記，然後是毛澤東與周恩來。在此之前，黨中央的常委會裡根本就沒有毛澤東。他是在遵義會議之後才被納入常委會。

根據李德在 1949 年離開中國之後撰寫的回憶錄，「毛並不遵守行軍的規定。他無精打采地在各個指揮部之間遊蕩，企圖說服每個指揮官採用他一己的想法。這麼一來，他讓領導地位變得很不穩定。」李德當時沒發現毛澤東正巧妙地嘗試逐一說服各指揮官為他的情勢分析背書，聯合反對三人軍事小組的勢力，最終讓他自己成為核心領袖。

遵義會議對中國與共產黨是福是禍仍有爭議。但是這

Line-up of members at meeting / 會議參與者一字排開

It was agreed upon that the meeting would only be for review of mistakes in militarily terms in order to determine the next path of action for the Red Army. No political issues were to be discussed. Zhang was first to pull the trigger in rigorously denouncing the wrong approach by the Three-person Group, elaborated by Mao's analysis of the current military situation. Mao further defined his unorthodox military strategy of evasive guerrilla warfare, manoeuvring to counter a much better equipped and numerically superior enemy.

A new core group of Three-person military leadership was established, encompassing Zhang Wentian who became General Secretary for the next eight years, Mao Tse-tung and Zhou En-lai. Before this point in time, the Standing Committee of the Central Party organ did not even include Mao. He was inducted into the Standing Committee following the Zunyi Meeting.

Busts of Zhou and Zhang at meeting / 會場的周恩來和張聞天半身像

個會議確立了兩個重大議題。第一，根據毛對紅軍現狀的分析而擬定短期戰略讓共產黨得以倖存。第二，開了個先例，以批判內部而造成領導人的更換。後者在紅軍以延安作為基地後的政治運動型態訂定了基調，其影響持續到中華人民共和國成立初期，以及文化大革命，直至今日。

至於我們這些凡人，仍將會在中國貴州省的這個角落，繼續閱讀或聆聽這個歷史重大事件的耳語。

Zunyi in the 1930s / 1930 年代的遵義

As Li De were to write in his memoir after leaving China in 1949, "Mao did not abide to regulations of a marching army. He was listlessly wandering from one army command to another, trying to convince and lure each commander to adopt his thinking. By doing this, he brought instability into the leadership." Li did not realize at the time that Mao was wisely trying to convince one commander at a time to endorse his assessment of the situation, and aligning opposition against the Three-person Group military command, and ultimately establishing himself into the core leadership.

Whether the Zunyi Meeting is a blessing or a curse for China and the Communist Party is debatable. But the meeting confirmed two major issues. Firstly, a near term military strategy based on Mao's analysis of the Red Army's status which allowed the Communist to survive into the future. Secondly, it sets a precedent for internal criticism resulting in change of command of leadership. This latter issue would set the pace for other political campaigns when the Red Army established its base in Yenan, and with implications throughout the early People's Republic, as well as into the Cultural Revolution, perhaps even to today.

As for those of us Fan Ren, or common people, we would continue to read or listen to the quiet whisper of this history making event, in a distant corner of Guizhou Province in China.

天坊

孫子我台

日月雙輝

天官賜福地主賜財

地靈人傑壽域光涵萬

流放與獄中的詩

POEMS IN EXILE AND IN PRISON

Danzhou, Hainan - March 9, 2017

流放與獄中的詩

蘇東坡和胡志明

羅浮山下四時春，
盧橘楊梅次第新，
日啖荔枝三百顆，
不辭長作嶺南人。

白頭蕭散滿霜風，
小閣藤床寄病容，
報導先生春睡美，
道人輕打五更鐘。

上面兩首詩出自蘇東坡（蘇軾），他與柳宗元、王安石（宋代的宰相）、蘇軾之弟蘇轍，還有父親蘇洵等名列「唐宋八大家」，而他有可能是其中最受到欣賞與景仰的文學大師。這只是他眾多優美作品裡的兩首，但作品也讓他遭遇到被外放的命運。

蘇東坡曾經是皇帝的中書舍人，但是後來失寵，被流放

POEMS IN EXILE AND IN PRISON

Su Dongpo and Ho Chi Minh

"Below Mount Luohuo four seasons all spring,

Orange and plum fresh they bring,

Three hundred lychee every day I consume,

Forever a person south of the range I assume."

"White hair loose like frost in wind,

Sickly looking I lay on a rattan bed on the loft,

Report that I am asleep like the grace of spring,

A passer-by with the bell of five o'clock softly rings."

The poems above are among many such beautiful writings that spelled further exile for Su Dongpo (also known as Su Shi), debatably the most admired and respected literary icon among the eight literary greats of the late Tang and early Song dynasties; including Liu Zhongyuan, Wang Anshi (a prime minister of the Song Dynasty), Su's younger brother Su Zhe, as well as the father Su Xun.

Hainan's Su Dongpo study / 蘇東坡在海南島的書房

到廣東省惠州，這時也是他寫下上面兩首詩的時候。他
被政敵陷害而被流放。被外放到南方的生活理應是艱辛
的，但是他詩中書寫的愉悅被政敵發現，透露出他在流
放中仍然自得其樂時，政敵很快地擬了一個計劃，把蘇
軾再往南外放，到更遙遠的海南島儋州。

竹外桃花三兩枝，
春江水暖鴨先知，
蔞蒿滿地蘆芽短，
正是河豚欲上時。

Su Dongpo at one time was a court tutor to the Emperor, yet fell out of favor and was exiled in disgrace to Huizhou in Guangdong by the time the above poems were scripted. Framed by his enemies, he was banished. Life deep in the south of the empire was supposed to be tough and bitter. Yet when his delightful poems were discovered by his rivals, revealing that Su was still enjoying himself in exile, another scheme was quickly devised, compelling Su to move further south, into even more distant Danzhou of Hainan island.

"Across from the bamboo two to three plum trees,
Warmth of spring river is noticed first by ducks diving free,
Dried weed on the ground as reed shoots are still short,
Just as the puffer fish is about to be served hot."

In those days, almost one thousand years ago, the island was noted for its hardship, barren but for beasts and malaria infestation; a land of no return. It was considered the final destination as hell for courtiers who fell from the Emporer's favor. Even Li Deyu, a former prime minister of the Tang Dynasty, was banished and died there. Yet Su wrote and exchanged over two hundred poems with his brother, who was also banished to nearby Guangdong province.

In all, Su Dongpo spent three years in Danzhou where he would usher in a new wave of scholarship and study. His modest home would be frequented by

在將近一千年前，海南島以困苦聞名，荒蕪之地只有野獸和瘧疾；是個不歸路。對失寵的臣子而言這裡像是地獄般的終點站。連唐代的宰相李德裕被流放到此也都在這裡喪命。但是蘇東坡在這裡又寫了兩百多首詩，寄給也被貶到附近廣東省的弟弟。

蘇東坡在儋州總共住了三年，在此引進學習研究的新浪潮。他的陋室經常有來自海口的學者來訪，海口是當時海南島最大的城鎮。後續的歲月中，儋州培養出許多通過科舉的學者，把有學問的人送進朝廷。

我在 1984 年卅多年前就去過海南島，最近十年間也去了十幾次，蘇東坡的故居離我們在鄰縣昌江的項目不到十公里，但是直到最近我才有機會去探訪他簡陋的住所。但是遲到總比不到好，最近這趟我終於去了蘇東坡住了三年的儋州朝聖。

這段期間寫的詩透露蘇東坡遙遙領先他的時代與大眾的想法，尤其是關於海南原住民黎族的尊嚴與平權等議題。他甚至在離開海南時寫給黎族的告別詩中，自我認為儋州人，說他的出生地四川只是暫住過的臨時居所而已。《別海南黎民表》，「我本儋耳人，寄生西蜀州。」

scholars from Haikou, then the largest town of Hainan island. In subsequent years, Danzhou was to produce many successful scholars in the imperial examination, sending learned men to the central court.

My visit to his exiled home came late, though I first came to Hainan over 30 years ago in 1984, and had made over ten visits within the last ten years, passing by less than ten kilometers from his humble abode on the way to our project site in the next county of Changjiang. But better late than never, I made my pilgrimage on this recent trip to visit Danzhou where Su Dongpo spent three years.

Poems written during this period revealed that Su was well ahead of his time and public sentiments, especially in according dignity and equality to the minority Li people who are indigenous to Hainan. He even went to extremes in his farewell poem to the Li people when finally departing Hainan, identifying himself as from Danzhou and portraying Sichuan, his place of birth, as just a temporary abode.

"Half awake and half intoxicated I ask the Li my way in wonder,
Bamboo thorny and rattan sharp every step I wander,
Looking for a lost cow I search for a way to get home,
My house and cowshed are still west of west."

半醒半醉問諸黎，
竹刺藤梢步步迷，
但尋牛矢覓歸路，
家在牛欄西復西。

蘇東坡天性樂觀，用正面態度接受他的流放，繼續寫出
一些他生平寫過最好的詩與散文。65 歲時，他終於獲
得朝廷的赦免，離開海南踏上漫長的返家之路。很不
幸，上路 6 個月之後他生病了，還沒回到家就過世了。

「橫看成嶺側成峰，遠近高低各不同」，蘇東坡是這麼
描寫他看到的山。

Always an optimist, Su Dongpo took up his exile residency with a positive spirit and continued to write some of his best literature, poems and prose. At the age of 65, he finally received court pardon and left Hainan to begin his long journey home. Unfortunately, after six months on the road he fell ill and passed away before reaching his home.

"Look broadside it is a range; observe from the side it becomes a peak, far and close high and low are not the same," So wrote Su Dongpo of the mountains he looked upon.

Not far from these peaks, across the Bay of Tonkin, is Vietnam and Guangxi Province of China. Back and forth along this border wandered someone less known as a poet, but much better known as a revolutionary and the founding father of Vietnam. Few know Ho Chi Minh wrote 133 poems - not in Vietnamese, not in French, but in Chinese, with perfect rhymes.

The poems were scripted while he spent slightly over a year in prison in Guangxi Province between 1942 and 1943. I had the privilege to visit a few places where Ho Chi Minh went through captivity. As he noted in one of his earlier poems,

"I've never been fond of chanting poems,
But in prison what else can I do in boredom,

Mountains of western Hainan / 海南島西部山脈

離這些山峰不遠處，北部灣對面，是越南和中國廣西省。沿著邊界來回穿梭的還有個比較不出名的詩人，但以革命家和越南國父的身分聞名。很少人知道胡志明寫過 133 首詩——不用越南文，不用法文，而是中文，還能夠押韻。

這些詩是他從 1942 到 1943 年在廣西省被囚禁一年多時寫的。我有幸探訪胡志明被囚禁的幾個地方。如同他在早期創作的詩中所說，

老夫原不愛吟詩，
因為囚中無所為，
聊借吟詩消永日，
且吟且待自由時。

在那個動亂時代，胡志明帶領叛亂團體滲透越南時，他的革命聯絡人多數都在中國。胡被決心消滅共產主義的國民黨抓到，監獄一間換過一間，最後終於被釋放。

不像一般囚犯，政治犯多是受過高等教育又具浪漫性格的，如同胡志明的另一首詩《夜晚》所述。

For long days I spend composing poetry,
Waiting for release to freedom".

In those heady days, most of Ho's revolutionary contacts were in China as he led his insurgent group to infiltrate Vietnam. Captured by the Kuomintang, which was determined to stamp out communism, Ho was transferred from prison to prison before being finally released.

Unlike common criminals, political prisoners tended to be far better educated and romantic, as depicted by another of Ho Chi Minh's poems; "Night".
"After dinner the sun sets to the west,
From every corner rises music of folk song fest,
Though dim, Chengxi detention dormitory,
Suddenly becomes an artist's academy."

Perhaps in anguish and longing for his Chinese wife in distant Guangzhou, Ho followed by penning the next poem, "Flute of a fellow prison mate".
"Nostalgic a flute wails in the ward,
Sad grows the tune and mournful the melody,
Thousands of miles beyond mountain passes and rivers melancholy,
A wife mounts a floor to gaze at distant territory."

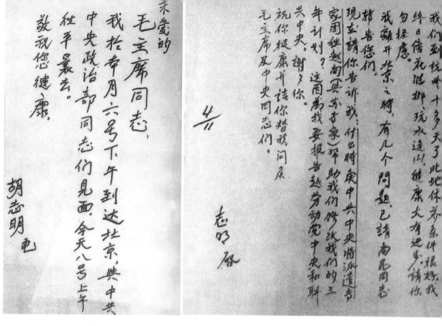

Handwritten letters to Mao & Deng / 寫給毛澤東與鄧小平的信

晚餐吃了日西沉，

處處山歌與樂音，

幽暗靖西禁閉室，

忽成美術小翰林。

或許痛苦又思念遠在廣州的中國妻子，他接著寫了這首
詩，《獄友之笛》。

獄中忽聽思鄉曲，

聲轉淒涼調轉愁，

千里關河無限感，

閨人更上一層樓。

His drama in the poem "Foot Lock" extended itself even to his chain of confinement.

"Frightful his hungry mouth is like that of a beast,

Each night gaping to devour the foot as a feast,

Its jaws swallowed the right foot of everyone,

Free to bend and stretch is but the left one."

On an exceptionally cold night, he remembered it again with a poem,

"Deep in autumn no mat and no quilt,

Bent waist with raised legs, sleep I try,

Moon shining on banana palm only adds more chill,

Through the bars the North Star already crossed the sky."

With irony, he wrote "Bound".

"Entwined round my arms and legs a long dragon,

Resembling a foreign officer with braids on his shoulders,

But the honored officer is decorated with golden silk thread,

While mine is a hemp rope made to make me dread."

In "Losing a Tooth", he wrote,

"You are tough and can withstand the test,

Unlike my tongue long and rather soft at rest,

Forever together we went through sweet and bitter times,

他在《腳鐐》詩中劇本進一步延伸到他的禁錮工具。

猙獰餓口似兇神，
晚晚張開把腳吞，
各人被吞了右腳，
只剩左腳能屈伸。

在一個特別寒冷的夜晚，他又寫詩回想，

秋深無褥亦無氈，
縮脛弓腰不可眠，
月照庭蕉增冷氣，
窺窗北斗已橫天。

他寫的《綑綁》帶著諷刺。

脛臂長龍環繞著，
宛如外國武勳官，
勳官的是金絲線，
我的麻繩一大端。

Now we are parted, one goes east, the other west."

In mundane and trivial objects Ho Chi Minh could also portray something po-
etic, as in "Listening to a Rooster Crow".
"You are but a simple ordinary rooster,
Every morning announcing sunrise with your calls,
Awakened from dreams, you announce for all,
That your service and labor is quite tall."

Ho Chi Minh's command of Chinese, both spoken and written, was superb.
But it was Cantonese in which he was most fluent. He was a fan of Canton-
ese opera. Even his only marriage, brief, secretive and kept off the record
in Vietnam, was to a midwife nurse of Hakka decent living in Guangzhou,
Tsang Xuming.

Perhaps asking how and why Ho Chi Minh became so prolific in Chinese may
be historically important. Suggesting an answer, or even in search of such an-
cestral truth, however may be politically sensitive. I shall leave this to future
generations with more wisdom than myself to tackle, and satisfy myself in
only appreciating his poetic qualities.

他在《掉牙》中寫道，
你的心情硬且剛，
不如老舌軟而長，
從來與你同甘苦，
現在東西各一方。

在世俗瑣碎的物品中胡志明也能用詩描述，如同《聽
雞鳴》。

Ho's Chinese calligraphy while in Guilin / 胡在桂林時寫書法

My choice of some of these poems, though imperfectly translated into English, is a tribute to a lesser known talent - the founding father of today's Vietnam. While Su Dongpo hailed from almost a thousand years ago, Ho Chi Minh is from the last century. Yet both set a unique example of perseverance and romantic optimism as poets during very trying times.

Ho with Cantonese opera star Hong Xian-nu / 胡與粵劇名伶紅線女（原名鄺健廉）

你只平常一隻雞，

朝朝報曉大聲啼，

一聲喚醒群黎夢，

你的功勞也不低。

胡志明的中文書寫與口語能力都極佳。但最流利的是粵語。他是粵劇迷。他唯一一段短暫、祕密而不見諸於越南史冊的婚姻，娶得是一位住在廣州的客家助產士，曾雪明。

追問胡志明的中文如何與為什麼變得這麼流利或許具有歷史重要性。暗示答案，或者去挖掘這些古老的真相在政治上都是敏感的。這個問題我就留給比我更有智慧的未來世代去解決吧，光是欣賞他的文采我就很滿足了。

我選的這些詩，雖然英文翻譯得不盡完美，但卻是向這位越南國父不為人知的另一個天賦致敬。蘇東坡活在將近一千年前，而胡志明是上個世紀的人，兩人都立下了詩人在困苦時刻展現出堅忍、浪漫又樂觀的典範。

Ho Chi Minh signed photograph given to a friend, now in CERS collection /
胡志明送給朋友的簽名照，現為探險學會收藏品

Guangxi near Vietnam border landscape / 廣西靠近越南邊境的景觀

雞足山神山 CHICKEN FOOT SACRED MOUNTAIN

Jizushan, Yunnan – April 10, 2017

雞足山神山

十二年一度的朝聖

「可是，可是⋯⋯我剛吃過雞腳，那是我最愛的港式點心。」我向好友丹增透露時有點結巴。丹增是位博學的仁波切也是退休的西藏省委副書記，他噁心地稍稍皺起額頭。接著他跟我說一件我完全不知道的事，縱使我以前來過雞足山兩次。

我初次來此是 12 年前，2005 年，同樣是雞年的朝聖之旅。然後我在 2007 年又來一次，陪伴幾位已經年過九十曾經飛越駝峰的飛行員友人。那次旅程是他們第一次在地面上看到了二次大戰飛行時從天上看過無數次的寶塔。寶塔是他們飛行時的參考點，飛越高聳的喜馬拉雅山脈之後指引著他們往昆明的方向飛去。

幾乎所有的漢人朝聖者，或像我這種觀光客，都會直接前往山頂上的寺廟和寶塔。在過去登頂可能要花一兩天，現在除了有鋪好的道路還有纜車，遊客只要再走短短一個多小時就能從山腳到達海拔 3248 米的山頂。

CHICKEN FOOT SACRED MOUNTAIN

A once-every-twelve-year pilgrimage

"But, but....I've been eating chicken feet, my favorite dim sim dish," I stuttered a bit as I revealed this to Danchen, my close friend. Danchen, a very knowledgeable Rinpoche and retired Vice Party Secretary of Tibet, wrinkled his forehead a little in disgust. Then he continued to explain to me something I was totally ignorant about, despite having visited the Jizushan, or Chicken Foot Mountain, twice in the past.

I first came here twelve years ago, during the last Year of the Rooster pilgrimage in 2005. Then I came again in 2007, escorting several Hump pilot friends when they were into their 90s. On that trip they saw on the ground, for the first time, the pagoda they had seen from the air uncounted times while flying during World War II. The pagoda was their check point, navigating them to Kunming after passing the high mountains of the Himalayas.

Practically all Han Chinese pilgrims, or tourists like myself, would head straight for the temple and pagoda on the pinnacle of the mountain. In the past it might take a day or two to scale the top. Today a well-paved road fol-

我們將寶塔和旁邊寺廟當作終點算是情有可原，因為它們從遠處看起來是最顯眼的物體。但對所有藏族朝聖者而言，他們來這裡是為了別的目的，相當隱密的，深藏在山上的垂直崖壁裡。藏族朝聖者不去山頂的情況並不罕見。

「要是沒有華首門，就沒有雞足山，」這句話丹增在我們停留山上的三天裡重複說了好幾次。他的意思當然是比喻而不是地理上的意義。雞足山這個名字源自山形的特徵，好像雞爪，三隻腳趾突出一隻腳趾在後。但是此山的名聲是衍生自藏人古老的信仰，佛祖釋迦牟尼的十

On top of Jizushan / 雞足山上

lowed by a cable car ride and a short hike will take visitors from the bottom of the hill to the 3248 meters top in slightly over an hour.

We may be forgiven for using the pagoda and its adjacent temple as final destination since they are the most distinct objects observed from afar. But for all Tibetan pilgrims, they come here for something else, something quite hidden, deep inside a vertical cliff face of the mountain. It is not unusual for a Tibetan pilgrim to bypass the summit altogether.

"Had it not been for Huashoumen, there would be no Jizushan," Danchen repeated this remark several times during the three days we were together

View of top from pagoda / 從寶塔上俯瞰山頂

大弟子之一摩訶迦葉（*Mahakasyapa*）曾經到此傳教，然後脫掉僧袍在山上的陡峭崖壁裡打坐。

於是抵達的隔天早上，丹增帶我到山頂下方約 150 米處的華首門。這時才剛過早上九點，我們遇到很多藏族朝聖者但是少有漢人。藏人大多是身穿藏紅袍的喇嘛和尼姑。他們來自青藏高原各地區，西藏、青海、甘肅、四川和雲南。

幾位藏族婦女正在供奉氂牛奶油，將它塗抹在崖壁上。懸崖底端有個小壁龕，有水滴流下。喇嘛、尼姑和俗人等藏人都把手伸進去沾水，然後把幾滴聖水抹在眼睛上，據說這樣可以改善視力。有兩位尼姑想要多收集幾滴聖水帶回家給朋友。視力衰退中的我也在眼睛上大抹特抹。

有個高瘦穿灰袍的漢人尼姑一直在懸崖前跪拜。她來自附近的大理古城，五年多以來天天在此跪拜，每晚才回到山下的一間小屋。我問她藏人用作供品的白圍巾哈達（*kharta*）是怎麼掛在這座 40 米高的「門」上，而「門」，又坐落在二十幾公尺高的垂直岩壁之上。是不是用梯子或徒手攀登上去？「沒有，他們只是將大麥或沙子包在哈達裡然後往上丟。不知何故它就會黏在岩壁上，」她

in the mountain. Of course he meant it figuratively rather than literally in geographic terms. The name Jizushan came from the mountain's physical features, resembling the foot of a chicken with three toes protruding forward and one aft. But the fame of the mountain was derived from an ancient Tibetan belief that Jaiye (Mahakasyapa), one of the ten principal disciples of Buddha Sakyamuni, came here to preach, then took off his monk's robe and meditated inside a precipitous cliff face of the mountain.

So with this notion Danchen led me the morning after my arrival to this Huashoumen (men meaning gate), some 150 meters below the peak of the mountain. It was only a little after 9am and we ran into many Tibetan pilgrims but few Han Chinese. Among Tibetans, most were monks and nuns in their saffron robes. They came from all regions of the plateau, Tibet, Qinghai, Gansu, Sichuan and Yunnan.

A few Tibetan ladies were making offerings of yak butter, rubbing it onto the cliff face. There is a small niche at the bottom of the cliff. Inside there was a little water dripping. Tibetans - monks, nuns and lay people - dipped their fingers inside and brought out sacred droplets to rub over their eyes, supposedly most auspicious for their eye sights. Two nuns were trying to collect a few more droplets to take home for friends. I, with deteriorating eye sight, applied droplets generously to my eyes.

平靜地低聲回答。看在她這麼虔誠,我傾向於相信她。

據說來雞足山的朝聖者如果看到神聖的雲朵和其他自然現象出現就會行大運。我在山頂上和華首門都看到了這樣壯麗的景觀,我自認也很幸運。

要描述聖地華首門,我就要借用十七世紀明末徐霞客的話。對我們漢人來說,徐霞客是幾百年來最重要的旅遊作家。他來過雞足山兩次,每次都停留幾個月。他的代表作品《雞足山志》早已失傳。然而在他其他的旅遊作品中,曾經描述到他在雲南的期間,包括造訪雞足山。

「……貼著懸崖的山路越來越窄;往上看不到頂令人

Sacred eyedrop niche / 壁龕流出神聖的眼藥水

A thin and tall Chinese nun in a gray robe was prostrating continuously in front of the cliff. She was from nearby Dali old town and had been prostrating here everyday for over five years, returning each night to a small hut a bit down the hill. I asked her how the kharta, white ceremonial scarves used by Tibetans as offerings, were put high up on the perpendicular cliff, reaching over 20 meters up on this 40 meters high "gate". Did they use a ladder or free-climb up there? "No, they simply wrap it with some barley grains or sand and swing the scarf upward. Somehow they would stick to the wall," she answered with a calm and quiet tone. I am inclined to believe her, given her devotion.

It is said that pilgrims to Jizushan would be lucky if they were to see sacred clouds and other natural phenomena on display. So I too consider myself fortunate in viewing such majestic view while on top of the mountain as well as from Huashuomen.

Monks applying sacred eyedrop / 喇嘛塗抹神聖的眼藥水

發抖，往下看就像俯瞰深不見底的地獄。就像一幅萬尺卷軸畫掛在懸崖上。於此山中，很難判斷自身位置……懸崖如階梯往上延伸，屋簷凸出，盤旋向下……岩壁宛如關閉的門，上方有岩齒……高達兩百呎，上面是遙不可測的更高處……這就是華首門。」

但對我來說，或許最感人的字眼不是來自於山，也不是在那個年代約 108 座寺廟的描述。而是徐霞客長途跋涉到雞足山做的一件事。當年有兩人與徐同行，他的書僮和他的好友靜聞和尚。打坐誦經二十年，靜聞刺破手指用鮮血抄了一部《法華經》，希望有一天能把這部經獻給雞足山的寺廟。他們從靠海的江蘇省一起前往在雲南的這座山。

但是沿路，他們被搶劫了三次。最後一次在湖南，靜聞遭到盜匪重傷而喪命。當天晚上，徐霞客失眠徹夜寫了六首詩紀念他的好友。他的竹匣行李底下帶著靜聞的骨灰，走了五千多哩，約 2500 公里，前往雞足山。他在此把靜聞抄寫的血經獻給悉檀寺，把骨灰埋在文筆峰。

中國史上最有名的旅遊作家徐霞客的這個友情義舉，在雞足山永垂不朽。或許對我們與未來的世代來說，

In describing the sacred gate of Huashuomen, I would borrow the words of Xu Xiake of the late Ming Dynasty during the 17th Century. For us Chinese, Xu has been known as the most important travel writer throughout the centuries. Xu visited Jizushan twice, staying for months each time. His definitive written account, an Almanac on Jizushan, has long been lost. However in his opus work on his life-long travels, there are descriptions of his time in Yunnan, including his visit to Jizushan.

"...the path against the cliff becomes narrower and narrower; looking up shivering one cannot see the top, looking down is like peeking into hell without seeing its bottom. Like a painting of a ten thousand foot wall scroll hanging upon the cliff. Encompassed within this, its difficult to tell where the body belongs...The cliff appears in flight going upward, high with an eave extension, wrapping around downward...The wall face is like closing doors, with rock teeth above...with height of two hundred feet, above that are unmeasurable additional heights... this is Huashoumen."

But for me, perhaps the most moving words are not from the description of the mountain, nor about all the temples, some 108 in all during the ancient days. It is about a deed that Xu Xiake performed on his long journey to Jizushan. Traveling with Xu were two other persons, his book-carrier boy and his dear friend Monk Jingwen. Meditating and praying for twenty years, Jingwen wrote a copy of the Buddhist Fahua Sutra in red by poking his finger to script

到佛教神山朝聖的同時，這個忠實友誼的故事也應該
被牢記，成為我們對心靈世界的敬意。

朝遊雞足山，暮訪華首門，日月伴星辰，迦葉在其間。

Danchen praying / 禱告中的丹增

it in blood, hoping someday to offer the manuscript at a temple in Jizushan. Together they made the journey from Jiangsu in the coast toward the mountain in Yunnan.

But along the way, they were robbed three times. During the last episode, while in Hunan, Jingwen was critically injured by the robbers and died as a result of the incident. That evening, Xu lost sleep all night and wrote six poems in memory of his dear friend. He carried in the bottom of his bamboo pack the bone ash remains of Jingwen and traveled for over 5000 li, or 2,500 km, to reach their joint destiny of Jizushan. There he offered up the blood sutra of Jingwen at Xitan temple and buried the ash remains at Wenbi Peak.

Such an act of friendship is immortalized in Jizushan by Xu Xiake, the most famous travel writer of China's past. Perhaps for our generation as well as future generations, while making pilgrimage to a sacred Buddhist mountain, this story of faithfulness and friendship should also be remembered and become part of our tribute to the spiritual world.

探險用行李箱

EXPEDITION LUGGAGE ANTICS

Milan – April 25, 2017

探險用行李箱 我與旅遊良伴的漫長旅程

「我最新的行李箱是附睡袋的伸縮式床鋪，很適合剛剛離婚被老婆趕出家門的人。」馬克・薩德勒露出大大的微笑說。他說的是由他設計的這款超好看鋁製行李箱，屬於 *FPM Bank* 系列，才剛在米蘭設計週首次亮相。兩週前他把寢具加進了包括工作站（*Workstation*）的系列中，那款是附伸縮式桌子與帆布折疊椅的行李箱。

「是啊，我們產品一放到展示場上就馬上收到訂單。」馬克又說。米蘭是時尚、珠寶、家具、飾品等設計重鎮。馬克寬敞活潑的工作室靠近米蘭運河，是一棟擁有豪華中庭的花園建築，他的工作室還有個地下室，我們在這裡與他見面。他的住家就在隔壁的大樓裡，外觀現代化，但牆上爬滿了長春藤等爬藤植物。

「我們在倫敦哈洛德百貨展示了工作站（*Workstation*），以及這一系列的行李箱。有個顧客一看到就想買，但是

EXPEDITION LUGGAGE ANTIC

Odyssey of my traveling companions

"My latest luggage addition of a pull-out bed with sleeping bag is perfect for the newly divorced guy when his wife kicks him out of the house," said Marc Sadler with a big smile on his face. He is talking of the FPM Bank Collection, a superb looking set of aluminum luggage that he designed and had first shown at the Milan Design Week. Just a couple weeks ago he added the sleeper item to his original genre which included the Workstation, a luggage with a pull-out desk and canvas folding chair.

"Ah yes, and we are receiving orders as soon as we put the piece in the showroom," Marc added. Milan is the epicenter for designers, in fashion, jewelry, furniture, accessories, and more. Our conversation took place in Marc's colorful loft studio with a basement, at a tony courtyard complex near the canal of Milan. His home is in an adjacent building, modern looking, yet with ivy and other climbers greening the outside.

"We have a Workstation on display at Harrods, together with our entire line of luggage. A customer wanted to purchase it upon seeing it. But if sold, the at-

如果賣掉，展場的吸引力就會減弱，所以我拒絕了。」
馬克回憶此事時顯然很驕傲他並不是完全被市場拉著
走。接著他把行李箱原型樣板推過來，告訴我原型設計
細節上的問題而他又是如何解決它們的。

這正是我對有理想性的藝術家的期待，不像當代所謂的
「藝術家」，已經被市場經濟汙染敗壞。價格無疑已經
成為名氣與美感的指標，而馬克・薩德勒的行李箱屬
於高端的，兼具功能與美感，而非只是為了索取天價在
作品上加個名牌而已。

這個鋁製行李箱有個高科技工業造型，不僅有個蝴蝶造
型的鎖，皮革握把更增添了古典美。行李箱主體在義大
利製造，輪子則是在日本設計與製造。為了環保，使用
回收的鋁。我第一次看到它是走出米蘭機場大門時，在
廣告看板上看到的。品牌很好記，FPM，意思是米蘭皮
革工廠（*Fabbrica Pelletterie Milano*），但是拼字和發音
都有點難。

住進飯店之後，我上網搜尋發現這家公司在米蘭，有家
門市離主教座堂廣場很近。於是我出門去找這家店。原
來這家店面相當小，在史卡拉歌大劇院附近。櫥窗裡就

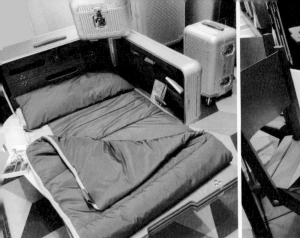

Sleeper and Workstation luggage / 寢具行李箱 · 工作站行李箱

traction would be diluted, so I said no." Marc recounted this with obvious pride in not being all market-driven. Then he wheeled over the original prototype of the luggage, and explained to me some of the issues in design details and how he had solved them.

That's exactly what I would expect from an artist with high ideals, unlike the so-called "artists" of the contemporary world, polluted and corrupted by the market economy. No doubt price mark has become a measure of fame and beauty, and Marc Sadler's luggage is right up there, yet both functional and beautiful, rather than just adding a label to design in order to command astronomical prices.

This aluminum luggage with butterfly locks offers a hi-tech engineering form and look, yet with a touch of classic balance with its leather handles. The main body is made, or tooled, in Italy, with wheels engineered and crafted in

是那個附帶伸縮式床鋪跟睡袋的行李箱。

跟店員一聊，原來這是 FPM 唯一的一家零售門市。馬克・薩德勒設計的 Bank 系列是他們幾位名設計師作品中的最新力作。然而，他們倒是透過在日本與上海的高級的零售店銷售，自從這個新的 Bank 系列上市之後業績可說是蒸蒸日上。

仔細檢視行李箱之後，我判斷即使在極端的環境下，它會比我用過的其他行李箱更能夠給予特殊器材與裝備提供更佳的防護。所以我決定買兩件……來測試它的能耐。我必須承認確實是它堅固又迷人的外觀讓我從口袋掏出兩千多歐元。

我並不習慣花這麼多錢買行李箱，不只因為探險學會這類的「設備」通常有人贊助，許多頂尖的戶外用品公司會為我們的需求特製行李箱。我於是想起了那些特殊的行李箱曾經陪伴我出門遠征跟旅行的那些時光。

我記得為美國國家地理雜誌探險時，我們也用過鋁製行李箱；Halliburton 公司製造、上開的鋁箱。箱子能夠隔熱，很適合放底片和攝影器材。我旅行通常會帶著幾件

Japan. And to be environmentally friendly, it uses recycled aluminum. I first set eyes on it in an advertising billboard as I exited the door of the Milan Airport. The brand is easy to remember, FPM, standing for Fabbrica Pelletterie Milano, something both difficult to spell and to pronounce.

After checking into the hotel, I checked online and found out the company is based in Milan, and with a shop quite close to the Cathedral at Piazza Duomo. So off I went, looking for the store. It turns out to be a rather small shop, somewhere near La Scala. In the window is the bespoke luggage with the pull-out cot and sleeping bag.

Speaking to the keeper, I found out this is the only retail store for FPM, the luggage brand. The Bank Collection designed by Marc Sadler is their latest addition to a handful line of designer luggage. However, they do have outlets through established high-end shops in Japan and Shanghai and business has been picking up ever since this new Bank Collection was launched.

After examining the luggage carefully, I decided it would offer adequate protection for special equipment and gear even on extreme expeditions, more so than some other luggage I've been using. I decided to purchase two pieces ... to test its resilience. But I must admit that the sturdy and attractive look helped nudge me to parting with over 2000 Euros.

這種好看的箱子，上面扣鑲著美國國家地理雜誌的黃色小標誌。攝影師偶爾會抱怨上面貼著大大的黃色標誌反而會吸引小偷偷走這些昂貴的設備箱。

1985 年長江探源時，*Wayne Gregory* 提供了專為我們設計與製造的大型背包。還給我們一些非常堅固的新開發布袋，大到可以裝下 25 匹馬力的舷外馬達。這些年來，我們使用過特殊規格的行李袋跟裝備箱，包括來自擁有 *Jansport* 的 *Whittakers* 集團；湯森兄弟創立的 *Wilderness Experience* 品牌；還有 *The North Face* 前任的老闆 *Bill Simon*；甚至 *Rick Ridgeway* 特製的橘色 *Patagonia*

I'm not used to paying so much for luggage, as not only was such "equipment" usually sponsored for CERS, but many leading outdoor companies have specially made luggage for our use. My memory went back momentarily to all the special luggage that has joined me on expeditions and travels.

I remember on my National Geographic expeditions, we also used aluminum luggage; top-loaded cases made by Halliburton. They are insulated and ideal for film and camera equipment. I generally travelled with several of these nice-looking pieces, with a tiny National Geographic yellow tag riveted to the top. Photographers occasionally complained that having a larger yellow tag would attract thieves to run off with these valuable equipment cases.

On my 1985 expedition on the Yangtze, it was Wayne Gregory who provided our sizable backpacks, which he designed and engineered. He also gave us some very sturdy duffle bags, large enough even to put our 25HP outboard motor in. Over the years, we had special luggage bags and equipment cases from the Whittakers, who owned Jansport, the Thomsens, who founded Wilderness Experience, from Bill Simon, former owner of The North Face, and even special orange Patagonia duffle bags arranged by Rick Ridgeway. Alan Uke who is a pioneer in waterproof cases and founder of Underwater Kinetics provided our equipment cases. At one point, good friend David Chu who founded Nautica designed special T-Tech duffle bags for us during the time

Various Tumi T-tech luggage / 各式 Tumi 公司 T-tech 行李袋

防水布袋。防水行李箱先驅與 *Underwater Kinetics* 品牌創立者 *Alan Uke* 也提供過我們的裝備箱。甚至連創立 *Nautica* 的好友 *David Chu* 在 *Tumi* 公司主管設計部門時還特別為我們設計了 *T-Tech* 防水布袋。

我記得很清楚在美國國家地理雜誌備受尊敬的攝影主任 *Bob Gilka* 跟我說過：「*HM*，如果需要什麼東西，就用買的吧，不要接受贈品！我們不想欠別人人情。」當時雜誌的銷量很不錯，*1980* 年代初期有一千多萬訂戶，一整頁的廣告要價十萬美元。但我一向認為最頂尖的「最好的」是買不到的。特別特製或是測試樣板

Halliburton & Jansport on camel /
駱駝背上的 Halliburton 與 Jansport 產品

while he headed design at Tumi.

I remember well what Bob Gilka, the respected Director of Photography at the National Geographic, told me. "How Man, if you need anything, buy it. Don't take freebies! We don't want to feel obligated." That was at a time when the magazine was riding high, in the early 1980s, with over 10 million subscribers and a full-page ad costing USD100K. But I have always believed that the "best" of the best, you cannot buy. Custom-made or prototypes for testing, is the norm for the explorer type.

25 years ago, I began using Zarges and Rimowa, both aluminum luggage made in Germany. In those days, to find any special case, I had to pick them up during my occasional lecture tour to Europe. Today, these cases are scattered around our many CERS project sites, including on our exploration boats in Myanmar and on Palawan in the Philippines. The Zarges are so strong that, on checking in at the airport in Myanmar, the airport counter staff refused to put them in as regular luggage, for fear of damaging other softer luggage in the airplane hold.

Many models of the Rimowa I used have since become vintage and obsolete in the market. But some of these luggage, formerly used by a select and exclusive few, have gone mainstream and become both fashionable and a status symbol. A year ago at the Hong Kong airport, I even took, by mistake, someone else's

原型製品才是適合探險家的。

25 年前，我開始使用 *Zarges* 和 *Rimowa*，這兩個都是德國的鋁製行李箱。在那個年代，為了找特殊的行李箱，我得趁去歐洲巡迴演講時順便採買。如今，這些箱子分散在探險學會各國的項目基地，包括我們在緬甸與菲律賓巴拉望的探險船上。*Zarges* 的產品堅固到在緬甸機場登機時，機場櫃員拒絕將它當作一般行李託運，深怕它會弄壞機貨艙裡其他較軟的行李箱。

我用過的許多 *Rimowa* 款式現在都已經成為古董在市場上絕跡了。以前這些行李箱只有少數特定人士使用，現在這個品牌已經進入主流市場，成為時尚與身分的象徵。一年前在香港機場，我還拿錯了別人的 *Rimowa* 行李箱，誤以為是我助理的。他發現後在深夜送還到機場，對方正在失物招領櫃台，還向她不斷道歉說是他拿錯了行李呢！

鋁製行李箱現在已經充斥機場，該是改變的時候了。所以對我來說，這兩件新的 *FPM Bank* 行李箱應該會在世界各地的機場引人注目，尤其抵達香港機場時，所有擠在行李提領處的鋁製行李箱主人都會向我的行李箱投來羨慕的眼光。我終於找到一個正當的理由讓行李箱在輸

Rimowa luggage, as I thought it was the one belonging to my assistant. When he found out and returned to the airport late in the evening, another person was at the lost and found counter, apologizing profusely to her that he had taken her luggage by mistake!

With aluminum luggage now flooding the airport, it is time for a change. So for me, my two new pieces from the FPM Bank Collection should soon be raising eyebrows at airports throughout the world, especially when I arrive at HK International, where the owners of all the other aluminum luggage coming out on the belt will be casting envious eyes on my pieces. For once, I have found a legitimate reason to let my luggage perform their cat walk for a second round on the conveyor belt.

This is a far cry from 1975 when I arrived in South America with a red, frame backpack. I had just left our VW van in Panama, on my first extended expedition driving from Toronto Canada through the Pan-American Highway to Central America, and was travelling onward to South America on foot. That

VW van circa 1975 / 福斯廂型車約於 1975 年   HM with backpack /HM 與背包

送帶的伸展台上多繞一圈了。

比起 1975 年我揹的紅色支架式背包抵達南美洲，真是
大不相同了。還記得那時我把福斯廂型車留在巴拿馬，
那是我第一次進行長途探險，從加拿大多倫多沿著泛美
公路一路開到中美洲，然後繼續步行到南美洲。那一趟
旅程持續了將近八個月。

如今四十多年過了，我的行李仍然繼續它的旅行，只
是風格變了。回到米蘭，與馬克・薩德勒訪談結束時，
他提議開車送我回飯店。但那裡離飯店有好一段距離，
我說我搭計程車好了。「沒關係，」他說，「我剛好
也要出去幫家人買冰淇淋。」這樣聽起來，他應該暫
時還不會需要用到自己設計的寢具行李箱吧。

first expedition had lasted almost eight months.

Now over forty years later, my luggage journeys on, though in different style. Back in Milan, at the end of my interview with Marc Sadler, he offered to drive me back to my hotel across town. It was a long way and I offered to take a taxi. "No problem," he said. "I'm on my way to buy some ice cream for my family." With that note, it seems he won't be needing his own Sleeping Luggage quite yet.

Marc Sadler at studio /工作室裡的馬克 • 薩德勒

到史特拉迪瓦里的故鄉朝聖

PILGRIMAGE TO STRADIVARI'S HOMETOWN

Cremona, Italy – April 24, 2017

到史特拉迪瓦里的故鄉朝聖

如果英文有「小提琴中心」（*violinocentric*）這個字的話，一定是指克雷蒙納這個位於米蘭南方搭火車需一小時的小鎮，據說這裡有超過 150 位小提琴製琴師。遊客去米蘭可能是為了 *Prada*、*Gucci* 和 *Armani* 等義大利名牌，然而全世界的音樂迷彷彿被磁力吸引一樣，到來克雷蒙納。在這裡肯定可以找到比全球化名牌流傳更久遠的品牌——史特拉迪瓦里、阿瑪蒂和瓜奈里，這些已經享譽三百多年的名匠名琴。這些小提琴的要價不菲，介於 1500 到 4500 萬美元之間，而且價錢必定還會繼續上漲。

如此天價讓現代的小提琴家和演奏樂手幾乎不可能擁有這些樂器。某位評論家曾說，「……小提琴家就像賽馬騎師，他們騎血統純正的賽馬比賽，但是卻沒有辦法擁有牠們。」幸好，許多名琴的主人會把琴出借給優異的樂手，有時候甚至出借一輩子，這也讓這些樂器可以一直保持在有人演奏的良好狀態下。僅有少數幸運的小提琴家在價格狂飆之前買到了自己的史特

PILGRIMAGE TO STRADIVARI'S HOMETOWN

If there is such a word as 'violinocentric,' it has to be about Cremona, a small town an hour by train south of Milan, purportedly with over 150 luthiers, or violin makers. Visitors may go to Milan in pursuit of Italian name brands like Prada, Gucci and Armani, but music lovers the world over are attracted, as if by the magnetic north of violin, to Cremona. Names that would certainly outlast globalized fashion names are found here - Stradivari, Amati and Guarneri, all known names for over 300 years. Prices of such named pieces are from the mountain tops, in the region of 15 to 45 million US, and will surely rise ever higher in the stratosphere.

Such prices make it next to impossible for violinists and concert artists to own such instruments today. In the words of one critic, "...violinists are like racehorse jockeys. They perform on thoroughbreds with pedigree, but cannot afford to own them." Fortunately, most owners loan their instruments to virtuoso to perform, sometimes for life, in order to keep such instruments in healthy condition. A few lucky violinists may have acquired their Strads or Guarneri before prices skyrocketed.

拉迪瓦里或瓜奈里琴。

如果史特拉迪瓦里有粉絲俱樂部的話，粉絲名單肯定就是小提琴家與音樂大師的名人錄。帕格尼尼（Paganini）、曼紐因（Yehudi Menuhin）、海菲茲（Jascha Heifetz）、史坦（Isaac Stern）、帕爾曼（Itzhak Perlman）、夏漢（Gil Shaham）、馬友友、貝爾（Joshua Bell）、穆特（Anne-Sophie Mutter）與諏訪內晶子（Akiko Suwanai）等名人，都只是名單的一小部分而已。我很幸運有三次機會在音樂會上聽過音樂家用他們最喜愛的名琴演奏。

我想去克雷蒙納很多年了，有兩次都計畫好了也訂了機票，但最後因為行程的關係而取消。終於，今年春天我利用週末在這個小提琴聖地待了三天。這趟旅行，我除了去看小提琴和製琴師之外也做了其他事。

自一月以來我兩次造訪菲律賓南部巴拉望島上正在消失的巴塔克叢林部落。我得知他們最重要財源之一是在叢林裡採集貝殼杉樹脂，俗稱馬尼拉硬脂。在販賣製琴師工具用品的商店「克雷蒙納工具」的網路型錄中，我發現了馬尼拉硬脂，應該是用在小提琴的表面塗層，但這個原料已經斷貨好一陣子了。我急著查明

If there is a fan club for Stradivarius, its members would read like a who's who of renowned soloists and concert masters of the violin world. Names like Paganini, Yehudi Menuhin, Jascha Heifetz, Isaac Stern, Itzhak Perlman, Gil Shaham, YoYo Ma, Joshua Bell, Anne-Sophie Mutter, and Akiko Suwanai are just the start of a star-studded list. I was fortunate to have heard three of them in concert, performing with their favorite instruments.

For years I wanted to visit Cremona, twice making plans and bookings, but aborting my trip due to schedule constraints. Finally, this spring I managed to spend three days over a weekend at this mecca for violinists. But on this trip, I am also on the trail of something else besides violins and luthiers.

Stradivari in front of his home / 家門前的史特拉迪瓦里

克雷蒙納和巴拉望之間的關聯，即使兩地遠隔著大陸與海洋。

小提琴上的表面塗層有很多製作祕方。安東尼奧‧史特拉迪瓦里那個時代使用的配方沒有被記錄下來，而配方之複雜無法被破解。但在一份古代手稿《亮光漆與奇特的祕密，克雷蒙納 1747》中，我讀看到關於配方的歷史也發現其中一些配方的祕密。重要的配方之一來自中國，簡稱為中國亮光漆，這個祕密配方由在中國傳教的耶穌會教士帶回歐洲。

無論是木材表面塗層或用在清潔繪畫用，有些配方好像是道聽塗說或民間傳說。 我在這裡引述一些例子：

不需要使用黃金來製造出金色
用磨成粉的番紅花、亮黃色的雄黃、野兔膽（用梭魚膽更好），混合之後放進玻璃瓶裡。將瓶子埋在馬糞裡幾天，然後取出來使用。

製造硃紅色
把燒焦的明礬小心地浸泡在玫瑰或車前草水中。最好是燃燒後立刻放進童子尿或酒精裡，或再加一些番紅花。然後跟徹底攪拌過的蛋白一起使用。

Since January I twice visited the vanishing Batak jungle tribe of Palawan in the southern Philippines. I learned that one of the most important cash products they collect from the jungle is the almaciga tree resin, more commonly known as Manila Copal. In the online catalogue of Cremona Tools, a shop that provides supplies to luthiers, I found the item Manila Copal, presumably used as an ingredient for violin varnish, but out of stock for quite a while. I am eager to find this niche connection between Cremona and Palawan though they are continents and oceans apart.

Violin varnish is made with many secret recipes. Those used by early luthiers like Antonio Stradivari were not recorded and can no longer be deciphered and replicated. But in an ancient manuscript, Varnishes and very Curious Secrets, Cremona 1747, I read about the history and found samples of such recipes. One such important recipe came from China, and was called simply Chinese Varnish. The secret was brought back to Europe by Jesuit priests, who learned it during their missionary work to China.

Some examples of concoctions, be they for wood varnish or cleaning of paintings, border on heresy or folklore. I shall quote some specimens. To make gold (color) with no gold,

> *Take powdered saffron, yellow and bright orpiment, a hare's gall (a pike's gall would even be better), mix well and put into phial. Bury the*

製造黃褐色顏料

盡量純化煙囪的煤灰，將其加入童子尿；放進玻璃杯中，注入清水。用棒子仔細攪拌，然後靜置。沉澱物落底後，將液體輕輕倒入另一杯子放置四天。沉積在杯底的就是最佳的黃褐色顏料。

清洗繪畫表面

混合灰燼、清水、尿液或白葡萄酒，抹在畫上，或將蛋白放在尿液中攪拌後塗抹在畫上，即可讓畫煥然一新。

這些來自 1747 年克雷蒙納的祕方讓我不禁懷疑馬尼拉硬脂，亦即巴塔克人的貝殼杉脂，會跟什麼原料混合在一起。我到飯店旁邊的史特拉迪瓦里廣場散步，逛到一

Violin varnish application / 小提琴上表面塗層
Peru Copal in market / 市場上的秘魯硬脂

phial in horse dung for some days. Then after a while, remove and use.

To make vermilion,

carefully imbue charred alum in rose or plantain water. It would be better to put it into the urine of a child or into aqua-vitae immediately after burning, or to add a little saffron. Use together with well whisked albumen.

To make bistre, a brownish yellow pigment,

Refine as much as possible chimney soot, adding to it the urine of a child; put it into a glass, fill it with clear water. Carefully mix using a stick, then let it rest. When most of the sediment has settled on the bottom, gently pour this liquid into another glass and let it rest for four days. What settles in the bottom of the glass is the best bistre.

For cleaning a painted surface.

Take ash, clear water, urine or white wine, and apply to the paintings, or whisk albumen in urine and rub over the paintings and they will look new.

Such recipes from Cremona in the year 1747 left me wondering what Manila Copal, or the Batak's almaciga, might be mixed with. While I strolled the Piazza Stradivari adjacent to my hotel, I wandered into a street market stall

個露天市場攤位，跟西班牙老闆買了一小袋祕魯硬脂。這是用來加入焚香以增添特殊香氣，傳統上人們相信它可以驅邪。不到一盎司重，就花了我四歐元。巴塔克人賣的貝殼杉脂，或馬尼拉硬脂，每公斤才六披索，等於美元二分。也許我快要嗅出這些叢林產品有更具產值的市場了。

我在週六抵達克雷蒙納時，大多數店家週末都沒有營業。到了星期一，我穿過安靜的小巷與無人的街道來到一處有大門的庭園。正門亮晶晶的銅牌上印著「克雷蒙納工具」，大門深鎖但有側門可以進入庭園。店門依然緊閉，但是擦亮的公司招牌底下有張紙用義大利文手寫，上面寫著一些日期，23 到 25 日，然後 26 日底下寫著一些字。

我用手機拍下，過街到轉角的咖啡店，年輕的女老闆會講一點英語。我把手機給她看問紙上寫些什麼。正如我所料，「23 到 25 日放假，26 日恢復營業。」這跟我的行程剛好衝突，因為我在 23 日抵達，26 日早上離開，回米蘭。所以馬尼拉硬脂之謎仍未解開。

我很沮喪，開始走回教堂所在的舊城中心。我的飯店離大教堂廣場只有一個街區。這兩天，我經過了七間製琴

and bought from the Spanish keeper a tiny bag of Peru Copal. It is used as a mix for incense burning, adding a special fragrance, traditionally believed to drive away evils. Weighing only a fraction of an ounce, it cost me four Euro. The Batak sold their raw almaciga resin, or Manila Copal, for a meager 6 peso per kilo, equivalent to 2 cents in USD. Perhaps I may be on the scent of a much more valuable market for these jungle products.

As I arrived in Cremona on a Saturday, most businesses were closed for the weekend. On Monday, I finally found my way through quiet alleys and empty streets to a gated courtyard. The shiny brass plate said Cremona Tools on the front. The gate was closed but a side-door led inside the courtyard. The door was closed, but under a nicely polished sign of the company was a handwritten paper in Italian with some dates, 23rd to 25th, then below it 26th something.

I took a picture with my phone and went across the street to the corner café, where the young lady owner spoke some English. I showed her my phone and asked what was on the paper. Just as I suspected, "Closed from 23rd to 25th, open again on the 26th." That perfectly conflicted with my travel plans, as I arrived on the 23rd, and would stay until the 26th morning when I would have to head back to Milan. So the mystery of Manila Copal would remain unsolved.

Dismayed as I was, I began strolling back into the heart of old town where the

Inside a luthier's workshop / 製琴師的工作室內部

師的工作室，因為週末連續假期，因此全都休息。

一條安靜的小街上，有個招牌指出巷子裡有位製琴師。
我輕鬆地走進去，驚訝地看到一道關上的門透出燈光。
我從玻璃門窺探，看到一位嬌小的女士正在桌前工作，
她手邊的木頭正被雕塑出小提琴的形狀。

我輕敲玻璃門，她抬起頭轉過來看著我，並起身開了
門。「我可否進來請教幾個問題？」我禮貌地問，並努
力擠出迷人的微笑。我帽子邊緣露出來的白髮想必讓她

Luthier shop / 製琴師的店

Cathedral was. My hotel was only a block from the Piazza Duomo. Over the
last couple of days, I had passed by seven luthier's workshops, all closed for the
long weekend holiday.

At a quiet side street, a sign pointed to a luthier inside an alley. I casually
walked in and was surprised to see a shop with closed door but with lights
inside. I peeked through the glass door and saw a petite young lady working
over her desk, chipping away at a block of wood the shape of a violin.

Tapping the glass door lightly, the lady raised her head and turned to look at

卸下戒心。「當然，請進。」她低聲說。

「我通常不會在假日進來的，但我碰巧早上 11 點有個約會。」她用清晰的英語說。「在這裡找到講英語的人真是太好了，」我驚呼。「你說對了，這裡的製琴師幾乎沒人說英語，也不會拉小提琴。」她微笑地回應說。「妳是哪裡人？」我問道。「我從以色列來的，在這裡當製琴師快二十年了，」她回答，「我當製琴師之前是位職業小提琴手。」她又說。

雅爾・羅森布朗不只是小提琴手兼製琴師，她還在《紐約時報》一篇關於克雷蒙納的文章中被提到，我在研究這個城市的時候讀過那篇文章。「我想請教關於表面塗層的事，尤其是樹脂的用法。」我直接問雅爾。「我已經不會自己調配了，太花時間而且很危險，」雅爾回答，「買現成的輕鬆多了。樹脂必須加熱到 330°C 才會融化，然後用來調配。它很容易著火，煙霧也很危險。我處理的時候必須戴著護目鏡。」雅爾繼續解說。

除了她的各種工具，我在她的牆上看到一批音樂 CD。「妳工作時會聽音樂嗎？」我問了個蠢問題。「我當然會聽音樂。」她回答。「使用工具時會聽搖滾樂嗎？」

me. *Momentarily she opened the door. "Can I come in and ask a few short questions," I politely asked, trying to put on a charming smile. The slip of silver hair peaking from the edge of my cap must have been a bit disarming too. "Sure, come on in," she spoke softly.*

"I am not supposed to come in on a holiday, but I happen to have an appointment at 11am this morning," she said in crisp English. "How wonderful to find someone speaking English here," I exclaimed. "You are right, hardly any luthier speaks English here. And almost none knows how to play a violin," she

Inside a luthier's workshop / 製琴師的工作室內部

我開玩笑問。「不可能，我只聽古典，」她嚴正地說。
我也趕忙正經起來問了些問題。她平均一年做五把小提琴；平均做一把琴要花上兩個多月的時間；完成一把之後才可以開始做下一把。製作一把大提琴則要花三個多月的時間。她做的小提琴經常在史卡拉大歌劇院演奏，一把好琴要價大約 12000 歐元。

我正準備離開時，問她是否介意用她的小提琴拉一曲作為壓軸。她同意了，於是從櫃子裡拿出一把漂亮的小提琴，纖細的手指在琴弦上滑動了起來。當我離開她的店走進巷子裡時，耳中仍縈繞著馬斯奈（Jules Massenet）冥想曲的柔和樂聲。

所有來克雷蒙納的遊客都應該去小提琴博物館看看，當然我也去了。我聽到大師用史特拉迪瓦里的大提琴 Chigiano 1682 演奏，這是克雷蒙納小提琴博物館的日常節目，演奏的樂器會從精細的收藏裡輪流挑選。真巧，為兩百多位觀眾表演安可曲時，他也是演奏冥想曲。我在書店買了幾本書和一本雜誌。《The Strad》雜誌裡都是關於史特拉迪瓦里樂器的故事，還有些是研究了幾十年才發掘出的事實。它創刊於 1890 年，現在已經是第 128 年。

said while returning a smile. "Where are you from?" I asked. "I am originally from Israel and have been here almost twenty years as a luthier," she answered. "I was a professional violinist before becoming a luthier," she added.

Not only is Yael Rosenblum a violinist cum luthier, she was even quoted in a New York Times article on Cremona, and I had read that article among other pieces in my research about the city. "I wanted to know something about varnish, especially the application of Copal," I asked Yael pointblank. "I no longer mix my own varnish, it is too time consuming and also dangerous," Yael answered. "It is far easier to buy it mixed. Copal has to be heated up to 330°C, before it melts, and then mixed. It is very flammable and the fume dangerous. I need to wear a goggle while handling it," Yael explained further.

Besides her assortment of tools, I saw on her wall a tidy roll of music CDs. "Do you listen to music while working?" I asked the obvious. "Yes of course I listen to music," came her answer. "Any rock and roll music while tooling?" I asked jokingly. "No way, I only listen to classical," she said firmly. I got serious and asked more relevant questions. She makes an average of five violins a year. It takes over two months to finish one before she starts another. A cello would take over three months to complete. Her violins are regularly played at La Scala, and a fine one would go for around 12,000 Euro.

As I was getting ready to leave, I asked if she would mind, as finale, play a

眾所皆知史特拉迪瓦里製造過 1100 多把小提琴和大提琴，其中有六百多把倖存至今。最新一期內容包括樹木年輪研究專家對第 26 號琴 Strad Paravicini 的鑑識報告。 它在幾乎全毀之後經過兩次的修復，現在又可以用來演奏了。

另一個專欄討論到小提琴家旅行時面臨的問題，因為他們的樂器可能會被海關官員用顯微鏡檢查是否符合國際瀕危物種貿易公約（CITES）禁用的 250 種紅木。而這

Modes an tools / 模型與工具

tune on her violin. She consented and took out a beautiful violin from a cab-

inet and began gliding her delicate fingers over it. I left her shop and headed

back into the alley with the very mellow sound of Meditation by Jules Mass-

enet still lingering in my ears.

All visitors to Cremona should visit the Violin Museum. I did likewise. I lis-

tened to a maestro performing on a Stradivarius cello, Chigiano 1682, a dai-

ly event at the Cremona Violin Museum, which rotates instruments played

from its very fine collection. Coincidentally, as encore to over 200 visitors in

the audience, he played Meditation as well. At the bookstore, I bought sev-

eral books and a magazine. The Strad is a magazine filled with wonderful

stories on Stradivarius instruments, some on facts dug up after decades of

research. It was started in 1890, now into its 128th years.

Stradivari is known to have crafted over 1,100 violins and cellos, with

more than 600 surviving to this day. The current issue included a foren-

sic report by a dendrochronologist, a tree-ring dating specialist, of Strad

Paravicini, or No.26, twice restored after almost total destruction, but

now again concert worthy.

Another sidebar discussed the issues facing traveling violinists, as their instru-

ments may be put under the microscope of customs officials to uphold regu-

lations under the Convention on International Trade in Endangered Species

種材料經常被用在樂器零件，例如小提琴弦栓。

克雷蒙納的亞洲遊客很少。有些日本人和韓國人會來這裡，特別是音樂家和音樂迷。隱密的小街角有個製琴師，*Rhee H. S. Pietro*。裡面有個亞裔年輕人在桌子上忙著工作。他的客戶有可能是他的韓國同胞。

日本的音樂基金會擁有至少 18 把史特拉迪瓦里琴。其中一把，*the Lady Blunt*，在 2011 年賣了 1600 萬美元為海嘯災民募款。割愛並不容易，但若是為了像這樣有義意的事，那就非常值得了。

近十年來在歐洲各大城市皆可見到大批的中國觀光客，但是在克雷蒙納幾乎看不到。但如果你網路搜尋「史特拉迪瓦里 小提琴 中國」，他們可是非常活躍。這個中國製造的網站列舉了好幾個這知名品牌的小提琴製造商。最暢銷的是 1715 型，最少的訂購量是 10 把！

兩年前，有一把史特拉迪瓦里琴，名叫 *MacDonald*，被拿出來拍賣。起標價是令人結舌的四千五百萬美元。雖然最後沒有拍出，未來如果有頂級的小提琴按照私人銀行家的建議淪為投資商品就太不幸了，他們會指點比較不懂文化的客戶把錢投資在名畫和其他藝術品。中國的

(CITES) against the use of 250 species of rosewood. Such material is often used in musical instrument fittings, such as violin pegs.

There were very few Asian visitors to Cremona. Some Japanese and Koreans have been known to visit, especially musicians and music lovers. On one obscure side street corner was a luthier, Rhee H.S. Pietro. Inside, a young Asian man was busy working over his desk. His clients were likely his countrymen from Korea.

The Nippon Music Foundation in Japan was known to own no less than 18 Stradivari. One, the Lady Blunt, was sold in 2011 for 16 million to raise funds for the Tsunami victims. A difficult parting, but for a very worthy cause.

Chinese seemed so far missing here in Cremona, despite swarming Europe's leading cities during the last decade. But if one were to Google 'Stradivarius violin China,' they are very much present. The Made-in-China site listed several manufacturers of the famed violin. Topping the list is a 1715 Model, with a minimum order of 10 pieces!

A couple of years ago, a Stradivarius, the MacDonald, was offered at auction. The reserve price was a jaw-dropping 45 Million. Though the lot failed to find a bidder, it would be unfortunate in the future if top violins were to become investment grade commodities, as has been advised by private

Cathedral Front Door / 大教堂的正門

bankers, who guide uncultured clients to put their money down on fine paintings and other objets d'art. The Chinese nouveau-riche would certainly not hesitate to speculate on such lots during auction.

A wealthy Taiwan collector has indeed degraded his four Strads to include them in a huge mosaic, or circus, of knick-knacks and animal specimens on display in his "museum". It seems that he bought his Strads just for the name, with a publicized aim of becoming the world's largest collector of violins. Such a notion should further distance him from those real connoisseurs with discriminating tastes who prize quality over quantity.

After five days of Italian meals since arriving in Milan, I was eager to find a Chinese restaurant. None were to be found within the vicinity of my hotel in Cremona. Across from my hotel, however, is a Sushi Bar/Restaurant. I settled with that for a change and ordered my meal. A young Asian lady in white, seemingly the chef, stopped by and asked me in rare English, "Where are you from?" "Hong Kong, most of the time," I answered hesitantly.

暴發戶肯定毫不猶豫地，不會錯失可以從拍賣中獲取投機的機會。

某個富有的台灣收藏家把他的四把史特拉迪瓦里琴降級，放在他的「博物館」，跟收藏的飾物和動物標本放在一起好像一幅巨大的馬賽克拼圖。他買史特拉迪瓦里似乎只是為了名聲，成為世界最大的小提琴收藏家。這種想法會讓他與真的會欣賞琴的行家距離拉開，真正的鑑賞家欣賞的是質感而不是數量的多寡。

抵達米蘭連吃了五天義大利餐之後，我很想找一家中餐館。我在克雷蒙納的飯店周圍都找不到。但在我的飯店對面有家壽司吧。為了換個口味我進去點了餐。一位穿白衣的亞裔小姐，似乎是廚師，走過來用鮮少聽到的英語問，「您是哪裡來的？」「香港，大部分的時候。」我有點猶豫地回答。

「喔，那你一定會講中文。」她用流利的普通話說。劉小姐五年前從中國沿海的浙江過來。前任老闆破產了，她跟兩個華人朋友頂下這家店。「再過兩年，我們打算改裝成中餐廳。」她說。看來中國觀光客湧入的日子似乎不遠了。

"Oh, in that case you must speak Chinese," she said in fluent Mandarin. Ms. Liu came five years ago from Zhejiang on the coast of China. The former owner of the bar went bust and she and two Chinese friends took over the business. "In two years, we intend to turn it into a Chinese restaurant," said Liu. It seems the time for the arrival of Chinese tourists will not be far behind.

Champion violins on display / 頂級小提琴

我的哈利波特時光
MY HARRY POTTER MOMENT

Cheltenham, London – May 3, 2017

我的哈利波特時光

與我在倫敦的祕密去處

我走進時管風琴的音樂充滿了整個大講堂。這座古典的三層樓「劇場」名叫公主廳，內部的空曠讓回音與共鳴更加響亮。巨大閃亮的管風琴，就坐落在三樓看台的全木質空間裡。

音樂突然停了。剛才有個女學生在排練聖詩，稍後她會在我開始演講前表演。我是在演講開始前過來檢查設備的。三十分鐘後，由女性組成的「唱詩班」合唱著讚美詩，頓時現場活潑了起來。

穿著體面的女孩們安靜地走進來就座。她們的制服是綠色外套加白上衣、深綠色方格裙，傳統又好看。還有幾位剛從運動會過來身上穿著運動服的孩子們。

楊（*Eve Jardine-Young*）校長身穿胸前有徽章的黑袍，走上舞台。她向大約 800 名女生說了些提要，然後簡單扼要地介紹我。語畢，有些好像安排好的掌聲響起。我上

MY HARRY POTTER MOMENT

And my London secret enclaves

The sound of the organ filled the entire auditorium as I walked into the hall. The emptiness inside this classic three-story "theater," named Princess Hall, made the echo and resonance even more pronounced. High up on the third floor balcony was a huge, shiny pipe organ, set upon an all wood surrounding.

Momentarily the music stopped. A student had been rehearsing a hymn that she would perform later before my lecture would commence. I was here to check the equipment before my lecture. Thirty minutes later, with the chorus of an all-female "choir" singing the hymn of thanks, the hall came to life.

That was, after well-dressed young ladies marched in quietly to take their seats. Their uniforms, jacket over a white blouse with a dark green skirt in check pattern, looked both conservative and smart. A few of the ladies were less formal in their sports jumpers, having just come from an athletic meet.

Eve Jardine-Young, the Principal, in a black robe with an emblem badge on the chest, got on stage. She addressed the 800 some young ladies with a few

台走到講台前，心想，這就是我的哈利波特時光，只差沒有魔杖或掃帚。

我轉身謝謝校長，又或者是「首席女巫師」，來回看著前面講堂滿是 11 到 18 歲的學生，她們的未來充滿了希望。這是個光榮又令人興奮的時刻。背景很完美。我突然變成了巫師，被這個中世紀氛圍迷惑。我想像蝙蝠倒吊在管風琴的巨大銀管槽裡。

這很符合邏輯與劇本。畢竟，JK 羅琳來自僅僅十哩外的格洛斯特郡。電影續集有些場景就在這附近拍攝的。

Principal of CLC / 切爾滕納姆女子學院校長

sundry reminders and essentials, then made a brief but to-the-point introduction about me. Upon that, and a somewhat orchestrated clapping of hands in welcome, I stepped on stage in front of the podium. This is my Harry Potter moment, I thought, though I was without a wand or a broom.

I turned and thanked the principal, or the "head witch", and looked up and down the hall full of future hopefuls, from 11 to 18 years old. It was an honorable and exciting moment. The setting was perfect. I was suddenly transformed into a wizard, but at the same time bewitched by these medieval surroundings. I imagined the bats hanging upside down inside the organ's gigantic silvery pipe silos.

It seemed logical and according to script. After all, J.K. Rowling came from Gloucestershire, just ten miles away. Some scenes of the subsequent films were shot in the neighborhood. The region had given inspiration to her stories, which captured the imagination of an entire generation, those in this hall included. They seemed to each have a secret part in her story, hidden to us outsiders.

Like a shaman performing his trade, my short film with heavy drum music transfixed them into a trance, bringing them along with me to a distant land, and a distant time from long ago. In fact, 30 years, 40 years, and longer, covering the time when I evolved from a child in Hong Kong through a growing

這裡啟發了她所書寫的哈利波特，並擄獲了整個世代的想像力，包括在現場的這些學生。每個人似乎都在她的故事中都有個不為外人所知的祕密角色。

如同薩滿施展魔法，我的短片配著鼓聲音樂，她們看得出神，彷彿被我帶到一個遙遠的地方，古老的年代。然而或許只有 *30* 年、*40* 年或者再久一點的歲月：從我還是一個小孩在香港長大到在耶穌教會念中學，隨後上美國大學，之後踏足中國做了四十幾年的探險與保育工作。這就是我的薩滿人生旅程。

我抬頭一看，學生們似乎真的被催眠了，還是在打瞌睡？但是如果她們在打瞌睡，眼睛怎麼睜得大大的。這是一所聲譽卓著的切爾滕納姆女子學院，簡稱 *CLC*，一所匹配得上未來國王的傑出學院，……不對，應該是匹配得上公主與未來的女皇。我在許多頂尖的中學與大學做過多次演講，從美國、歐洲、英國、亞洲甚至中東。但是這次不一樣。背景和學生穿的制服都讓她們與眾不同。

我的演講很長，將近一個半小時。這天是週六上午，學生們或許還沒有被課堂弄得精疲力盡。時間不夠我決定省略掉 *Q&A*。但我下台時，許多學生排隊等著要找我

process into high school, educated under the Jesuits, and later at university in America, before landing in China for four decades of exploration and conservation. Such was my shamanic journey of life.

I looked up again, and indeed the students seemed mesmerized, or were they half dozing off? But if they were dozing, they were wide-eyed. This was the esteemed and elite Cheltenham Ladies College, better known simply as CLC, an education pantheon fit for kings, ... no, I mean fit for princesses and queens-to-be. I have spoken to students of many leading schools and universities, both in America, on the Continent, the UK, in Asia and even in the Middle East. But this one was different. The setting and the ladies in stiff uniform made them special.

I delivered a long sermon, almost a full hour and a half. This was, after all, a Saturday morning, and the girls may not have been tired from classes yet. I ran out of time and decided to skip the Q&A session. But as I got off stage, there was a long line of students waiting to chat with me. These were senior girls, mostly ready to take on university and the world. Almost everyone was asking how to join an internship with CERS, to go along on the long journey I had described. I answered as best I could and handed out my business card for them to write to me, promising to consider their requests. Perhaps I should have asked them to make sure they tune-up their brooms before they join us in the faraway land.

聊天。這些都是高年級生，準備要面對大學與外面的世界。幾乎每個人都問我怎麼可以進探險學會當實習生，然後踏上我描述的旅程。我盡可能地回答，分發我的名片讓她們可以寫信給我，我承諾會考慮她們的要求。或許我該要求她們先準備好她們的飛天掃帚再跟我們去遙遠的國度。

我離開學校走進春寒料峭中，沿著河濱步道走一小段到市中心，鎮上只有一兩個商店街區。過街是個公園，裡面搭了大大小小的帳篷。人們漫步其中，這是一年一度的切爾滕納姆爵士音樂節。但之前的那個中世紀音樂仍然一直在我耳中迴盪著。我的車在我住的 *Malmaison* 飯

Colorful canal boats / 五顏六色的運河船

I left the school into the chill spring air and made a quick walk down the prom-
enade to the center of town, a town with only a couple blocks of shops. Across
the street in the park, big and small tents were set up. People were milling
around, as it was the once-a-year Jazz Festival of Cheltenham. But my ears
were still ringing with the medieval music of the theater. My car was waiting
outside the Malmaison Hotel where I stayed, and I decided to get back to London. There was another festival, also once-a-year, waiting for me.

Little Venice is not on many visitor's map or itinerary for London. But the
canals converging here near Paddington Station are the gathering point once
a year for the Canal Boat Festival. The long, narrow boats were here for the
weekend. Many were shined and polished to their best colors. Some people

Festive dress / 慶典服裝

店外面等候，我決定回倫敦。那裡還有另一場也是一年一度的慶典在等著我。

小威尼斯不會出現在倫敦的遊客地圖或行程上。但是匯聚在帕丁頓車站附近的運河是一年一度的運河船慶典所在。許多又長又窄的船隻紛紛來此聚集歡度這個週末。其中有很多船隻被擦亮拋光呈現出最美麗的色彩。有些人覺得住在船上很有樂趣。也有些人可能因為倫敦越來越高的房價而選擇住在船上。

船或許狹窄，裡面家居所需的設備可是應有盡有：臥室、客廳、廚房、衛浴，都設計得很舒適。有艘酒吧船，讓遊客可以品嚐二十多種啤酒。另外兩艘船改裝成餐廳，分別提供高端或經濟的餐點。

這個週末，有幾十艘船緊挨著彼此停泊，船上鮮豔的旗幟飄揚。船主們穿上各式各樣的服裝，從古典到現代，從紳士到海盜都有。搭篷的攤子，飲食攤，有旋轉木馬的臨時遊樂場，排列在停泊處的人行道上。甚至還有一家不動產仲介商，販賣全新或二手船，貼出漂亮的照片來吸引潛在的買家。下次來這裡我打算報名搭這種船遊河，自己開船，在英格蘭南部的運河迷宮中待個一週到十天。

find them a joy to live in. Others may have chosen to live on a boat because of the rising cost of flats in London.

While the boats may have been narrow, inside they were decked out with everything you could hope for in a home; bedroom, sitting room, kitchen, bathroom, all in comfortable setting. One boat was a bar, allowing visitors to sample over twenty types of beer. Two other boats were turned into restaurants, catering to both high-end and more budget conscious guests.

For this weekend, scores of these boats were parked closely next to each other with fluttering, colorful flags. Owners were dressed in an assortment of costumes, from classic to modern, and from gentlemen to pirates. Tent sale booths, food stalls, and temporary playgrounds with carousel and merry-go-round lined the sidewalk mooring for the boats. There was even a real estate shop, selling new or pre-owned narrow boats with pictures to attract potential buyers. Instead, I planned to sign up for a cruise on one of these boats, self-driven, for a week to ten days in the labyrinth of canal waterways around south England - for my next trip.

A short walk from the festival ground is the famous St Mary's Hospital of Imperial College. It is here where many members of England's royal family were born. Less well known is the Frontline Club across the street at the corner of Praed Street and Norfolk Place. Founded in 2003 by journalists

從活動現場走一小段路就是聞名的帝國學院附屬聖瑪麗醫院。許多英國皇室成員都在此誕生。比較不出名的前線俱樂部位於對面的普雷德街和諾佛克街路口。這個俱樂部是由記者們在 2003 年創立的，為了紀念因為工作而犧牲生命的戰地記者。

在中亞與中東衝突的高峰期，從 1970 年代末期的阿富汗到本世紀初的伊拉克，前線電視新聞提供了許多最即時的報導影片、照片和文章，他們的報導從衝突地區到世界各地。如今，大約有兩千名會員，多數是記者，立志追隨前輩的腳步，追求前輩們為這艱辛的行業所設下的高標準。

樓上酒吧與閣樓餐廳只保留給會員，但樓下的餐廳則對外開放，它的獲利用來支持俱樂部的運作。身為紐約的探險家俱樂部會員，我享有正式會員的權利，包括可以入住它的 12 間客房。酒吧的展示櫃裡有很多紀念品和罹難戰地記者的故事，或是九死一生的驚險故事。也有許多照片描繪戰爭前線的狀況，包括名記者羅伯特・卡帕（Robert Capa）在諾曼第登陸的灘頭所拍攝的系列照片。

客房樸實又舒適，每間都有一張放大的黑白照片佔據床

and for journalists, it is set up in memory of frontline war correspondents who sacrificed their lives in the line of duty.

During the height of the conflicts in Central Asia and the Middle East, from the late 1970s in Afghanistan to Iraq at the turn of the century, the Frontline Television News supplied many of the up-to-the-minute stories in film, photos and writings, from conflict zones to the rest of the world. Today, its two thousand or so members are mainly journalists, aspiring to follow in the footsteps of those who set the high standard that is the hallmark of a very trying profession.

While the upstairs bar and loft restaurants are reserved only for members, the downstairs main restaurant caters to anyone and, with its profits, benefits and supports functions of the Club. As a Fellow of the Explorers Club in New York, I can enjoy the privilege as a full member, including booking into its 12 guest rooms. The bar has display cases with many memorabilia and stories of these war correspondents who fell, or those who survived, barely. There are also many photos on display portraying highlights of the battlefront, including a series taken by Robert Capa on D-day at Normandy beachhead.

The guest rooms are simple and nice, each with a huge black & white photo taking up the entire wall against the head of the bed. Perhaps the only room to avoid is the one with a grim picture of fire burning during a volatile riot.

My new old books / 我新買的舊書

頭的牆面。唯一一間該避開的房間是有一張在暴動中烈
火燃燒的照片。對我來說，這些逼真的影像恐怕會讓我
失眠。有一張是在柏林牆倒下的前一天所拍攝的，許多
人攀爬在牆上的這張或許稍微好一點。

隔天是星期一，我在早上七點就抵達了柯芬花園。這已
經成為每次我在倫敦時，星期一早上的儀式。從早上
六點到中午左右，會有古董商人擺攤，但僅限週一。
過去，我在這裡挖到過很多寶藏，例如，雪菲爾的銀
器、維多利亞時代拐杖、探險望遠鏡、古董鐘，甚至
還有 1904 年西藏戰役中英軍頒給軍官與士兵的勳章。

在這個週一早上，我發現兩件老東西，都很適合放在探
險學會位於香港石澳的 1939 展覽館。一個是預測天氣

Items on sale / 出售的物品   Picture on display / 展示照片

For me, it would be a bit too graphic to go to bed with such images on the back of my mind. The one with bodies climbing up the Berlin Wall during its last day may be marginally better.

The following day is Monday and I head to Covent Garden, arriving at 7am. This has become my ritual whenever I am in London on a Monday. From 6am on, lasting to around noon, stalls are set up by antique sellers, but only on Monday. In the past, I have picked up many treasures, among other things, Sheffield silverware, a Victorian walking cane, an exploration telescope, a vintage clock and even English military medals conferred on officers and soldiers in the Tibet campaign of 1904.

On this particular Monday morning, I found two old items, both highly suitable for the CERS 1939 era exhibit house in Shek O Hong Kong. One was

用的溫度計兼氣壓計。另一個是還能用的老座鐘，上面還有發條旋鈕。這類骨董寶物不僅在香港很難找到，即使有也很貴。但是這兩件美麗的骨董總共才花了我40英鎊。

忽然，另一張桌上有兩本薄薄的書吸引了我的目光。《The Worst Witch》與《The Worst Witch Strikes Again》是系列童書的前兩冊，後來在英國翻拍成電視劇。作者是吉兒・墨菲，我看到的兩冊是1974與1980年的初版。吉兒這套書中的故事據說跟JK羅琳寫的哈利波特系列很相似，後者遲至1997年才出版。而兩位作家的書迷偶爾會在網路上辯論這些巫師故事的原創性。

但對我來說，我沒興趣參與這類關於真偽的辯論。在這個網路時代，幾乎所有知識和故事在網路上都是免費的。無論多古老的故事，都可以隨時被人改編。如果是好故事，像舊約聖經或古蘭經，或是佛陀或孔子的教誨，就會通過時間考驗反覆被傳述。

但現今高度商業化與金錢化的世界，成功地把每個人的故事帶入所謂的「智慧財產權」。這種行為究竟有多少智慧就讓別人去判斷吧。至於我，兩本我都買了，一本一鎊。開心閱讀巫師學校的故事時，我感覺又與

a thermometer with a barometer for weather forecast. The other was an old table clock that was still ticking, together with its winder key. Such old treasures are not only difficult to find back home, but very expensive if available. For me, the two beautiful pieces cost only 40 pounds total.

Suddenly, on another table two thin books catch my eye. "The Worst Witch" and "The Worst Witch Strikes Again" are the first two in a series of children's book that subsequently became a television series in the UK. Jill Murphy is the author and both copies I saw were first edition, from 1974 and 1980. Jill's stories in these books were said to have very close similarities with those authored by J.K. Rowling in her Harry Potter series, which came out much later in 1997. In fact, fans of both writers have occasionally engaged in debates online about the originality of these stories of witches and witches-to-be.

For me however, I have no interest of entering into such a debate of authenticity. In this internet age, practically all knowledge and stories are online, free. Adaptation of such stories, no matter how ancient, is up to anyone anytime. If they are good stories, like those in the Old Testament or the Koran, from the Teachings of the Buddha or Confucius, they would stand the test of time and be retold over and over again.

But today's highly commercialized and monetized world has succeeded in bringing everyone's story into what is called "intellectual property". How in-

兩天去演講的切爾滕納姆女校變得很貼近很緊密。下次我得查出學生們把魔杖跟掃帚藏在哪裡。或許憑著神奇的運氣,我也能成為巫師學徒。

Thermometer with barometer / 溫度計兼氣壓計

tellectual is such behavior will be for others to determine. As for me, I bought both books, one pound each. While enjoying reading the story of the school for witches, I feel connected again to my lecture two days ago at the Cheltenham Ladies School. Next time I must find out where the girls are hiding their wands and brooms. Perhaps with some magical luck, I can become an apprentice wizard.

達那寺

DANA MONASTERY

Nangchen, Qinghai – May 20, 2017

達那寺

擁有 1400 年歷史，葉巴噶舉派僅存的一間寺廟

我們在這高山深谷中好像迷路了。但我不會放棄，我們正在青海與西藏邊界尋找一座鮮為人知、失落許久的寺廟。

我們在前往西藏東南部尋找伊洛瓦底江源頭的路上繞了個路，很遠的路，但是找到這座獨一無二隱世的寺廟至關重要——這可是藏傳佛教的葉巴噶舉派唯一倖存的寺廟。

從玉樹往外的道路現在已經都鋪設柏油了，儘管如此還是要經過一些非常險峻的峽谷。在玉樹城外可以看到 2010 年大地震後的寺廟殘骸。但我們深感欣慰能夠幫忙資助玉樹重建一座古屋。

離開主要幹道之後的迷路也為我們帶來了驚喜，因為我們巧遇西藏僅存的幾座大型懸臂橋的其中之一。這座橋跨越偏遠的吉曲河，然後連結到湄公河的上游，是個名

Nangchen, Qinghai – May 20, 2017

DANA MONASTERY

1400 years old and last of the Yerpa Kargyu sect

It seems like we are badly lost among the hills and valleys. But give up I will not, as we are in pursuit of a little-known and long-lost monastery on the border of Qinghai with Tibet.

This is a major detour from our goal of reaching the source of the Irrawaddy in southeastern Tibet, but the stakes are high in finding this well-hidden monastery - last of a breed - the only surviving monastery of the Yerpa Kargyu sub-sect of Tibetan Buddhism.

The road out of Yushu is now nicely paved despite going through some of the most dramatic mountain gorges. Outside of Yushu we saw the remains of a monastery resulting from the disastrous earthquake of 2010. We felt a bit gratified that CERS was able to help fund the reconstruction of a historic old house in Yushu.

Being lost once off the main highway brings its own surprises, as we chance upon one of the very last sizable Tibetan cantilever bridges. Spanning the re-

符其實的古蹟，高原上這種橋梁早就消失了。

要是十年前尋找達那寺，得從玉樹開始騎馬加上走路，至少要花上三天的功夫。但是現在，應該是有條小路直接通到它門口，不過這條小路在哪裡？我們沿路問遍了大小村落。附近每個人都知道達那寺。大家都用神祕的中文說不遠！西藏版的「不遠」很像西藏人的「快了」或「只要一會兒」。

風景美得讓迷路都值得了。天氣好的時候這裡的石灰岩山彷彿高聳直入藍天。規模大的令人著迷，在這高海拔上令人眼花撩亂，我注意到有座石灰岩山腳有個大自然所雕刻出來的冥想小屋。霧霾飄來跟這些山玩起捉迷藏，只有這種景觀才配得上被稱作「景觀」。世界上越來越少有地方配得上「景觀」這兩個字了，因為大多被人為的加工所汙染了，而景觀的意思就是字面上那種純粹的意思。

在花朵盛開的草原上碰到幾條死路，還有一次走到村屋的圍牆邊，我們只好不斷地折返與尋找那條神祕的小路。一度，我們看到了兩座山峰，達那寺應該就在那兒，但我們卻在山的另一邊。走著走著遇到了一所綁著巨大兇猛藏獒犬的寺院學校，有個年輕喇嘛聽到

mote Jiqu river before it joins the upper Mekong, the bridge is literally a relic, as other specimens of this type of bridge have long disappeared on the high plateau.

Had I pursued this Dana Monastery ten years ago, it would have involved three days of hiking and horseback riding from Yushu. But today, a marginal road is supposed to reach its doorsteps. But where is this marginal road? We've been asking at villages and hamlets along the way. Everyone nearby knew of Dana Monastery. Everyone said in cryptic Chinese that it is not far away! The Tibetan version of "not far away" is not unlike the Tibetan time "soon" or "in just a short moment."

Earthquake devastated monastery / 被地震摧毀的寺廟

低沉的狗吠聲走了出來，終於碰到口中吐出的中文不是像謎一樣的人了；他真的懂也會說中文，在這個地區非常罕見。我們非常地感激，因為我們從詢問過的其他人口中只能分辨出 Dana Gomba 這個字，以及對方粗略的指引。

依照喇嘛的指示，我們爬上一個很高的山隘，確實有條小路出現眼前。越過隘口進入山谷，我們又迷了兩次路。途中我們還詢問了鋪路的工人，連他們也不知道寺廟在哪裡。這時剛好有個騎機車的阿尼路過，她的摩托車上還載了個乘客，出於好奇停下來看我們在幹嘛。

「跟我走，我也要去那裡，」功松庫吉說。功松不僅認得路，中文也講得很好！她在這些泥土路上騎車的樣子比較像越野賽車手而非身穿藏紅袍的阿尼。原來她後座的瑜珈修行者要到達那寺稍個口信。她的機車時不時地會停下來，她於是下車檢查油管。

「我剛剛才在一家小店加滿了油，肯定是加到摻水的爛汽油了！」功松大呼。她修好油管之後用腳發動了車子好幾次，動作一點也不像年輕的阿尼，倒像活力充沛的小男孩。我在一旁看著她，既羨慕也佩服，回想起自己

Detail of cantilever / 懸臂細部   Cantilever bridge / 懸臂橋

But the scenery more than compensates for being lost. The limestone hills are jettisoned into the blue sky when the weather is fine. The scale is mesmerizing, even mind-dazzling at such high altitude, as I observe tiny meditation huts in the foothills of a karst mountain sculpted by nature. Then haze and mist come in and play hide and seek with these mountains, in a landscape worthy of being called "landscape". Fewer and fewer places of the world deserve the word "landscape" today, as the human hand has touched , and in most cases contaminated, what the word was originally meant for in a literal sense.

After several dead-ends in meadows with flowers in bloom and one at a fence around a village house, and we are again turning back to seek the long sought-marginal road. At one point, we see the twin pinnacle peaks in whose foothills Dana Monastery is supposed to be, but we are on the wrong side of the mountain. At a monastery school, where a huge and fierce Tibetan Mastiff is tied, a young monk comes out upon hearing its baritone barking. For

Dana Hill and monastery from afar / 達那山與寺廟的遠景

年輕的時候騎著越野機車探索長江上游的情景。

「妳騎車技術好像專業賽車手。」我說。「我十幾歲的時候，不想待在學校裡，像個男生那樣到處玩耍，」功松說，「九年前我決定當尼姑，這樣才能離開學校。」她又說。現在她 26 歲了。很明顯地，她小時候一定像個小男生。

將近一小時後，功松帶我們進到一個水流湍急的山谷裡。從這裡我看得到遠方有座很壯觀陡峭的石灰岩山，雙子峰的形狀好像馬的耳朵。因此藏語名字才叫達那，「達」是馬，「那」是耳朵。有著紅牆的寺院群就散落馬耳朵下，位於海拔 4300 米處。這就是達那寺，終於近在眼前了。

達那寺有著很特殊的傳承故事。在 1188 年，這座寺院改成西藏教派其中之一的噶舉派，屬於白教。寺院創立者是桑傑葉巴，所以教派名稱變成葉巴噶舉。在那之前的 600 年，該寺一直是苯教寺廟，信奉佛教傳入前的西藏本土宗教。因此，達那寺被認定為西藏最古老寺廟之一，總共有 1400 年的歷史。

達那寺在 2006 年被指定為國家重點保護文化遺產。先

once no mere utterance of cryptic Chinese-like sounds; he actually understands and speaks Chinese, a rarity in this part of the plateau. It is much appreciated, as others we have asked could only make out the word Dana Gomba and point in a general direction.

We follow his directions and head up a very high mountain pass, a marginal road indeed. Over the pass and down into a valley and we are lost twice more. Finally, as we are asking some road builders, who have no idea where the monastery is, a nun with a passenger on her motorcycle stops out of curiosity to have a look at us.

"Follow me, that's where I'm going," says Gongsong Quji. Not only does Gongsong know the way, she speaks perfect Chinese! The way she rides her motorcycle on these dirt roads seems more like a dirt bike racer than a nun in saffron robes. She has a yogi on the backseat who needs to get to Dana Monastery with a message to deliver. Every now and then, her bike stops and she climbs off to check its gas feed.

"Must be bad gas with water. I just refueled a moment ago from a local shop!" Gongsong exclaims. She kick starts it multiple times after fixing the gas line, acting more like an energetic young boy than a young nun. I observe with envy and admiration, reminding myself of younger days when I took a dirt bike on excursion while exploring the upper Yangtze.

前它只是省級保護的古蹟。其中有一座特殊的建築，位於岬角上的最高處，被視為寺內最古老最有歷史的建築物。

對許多藏傳佛教徒來說，十二世紀在噶舉派下創立的葉巴次級教派據說已經跟其他教派融合了，早已不復存在。然而，很少人知道這個教派在高原偏遠角落的寺院裡倖存。所以達那寺在整個青藏高原上，包括中國境外的，數百或許數千座寺廟之中顯得非常特殊。

此外，達那寺也是嶺國的寺廟。嶺國的格薩爾王是西藏高原喀木地區的傳奇國王。他出生於長江上游金沙江畔的鄧科，現稱德格。他的啟蒙大師是桑傑葉巴，所以跟達那寺有淵源。格薩爾的王國叫做嶺國，打過許多場戰役統一了整個地區，所以他號稱是西藏史上最出色最勇敢的戰士。達那寺應該是唯一格薩爾參拜過還存留的

Tibetan mastiff / 西藏獒犬

"You ride like an expert racer," I comment. "When I was a teenager, I did not want to stay in school and played like a boy," Gongsong says. "I decided to become a nun nine years ago so I could leave school," she adds. Today she is 26 years old. Obviously, she must have been a tom-boy in her younger days.

It takes almost an hour for Gongsong to lead us down a ravine into a valley with a fast flowing stream. From here, I can see far off at the foot of the valley a most spectacular and precipitous limestone hill, with its twin peaks shaped like a horse's ears. Thus the name Dana in Tibetan, "Da" meaning horse and "Na" ear. Below it are specks of monastic buildings with red walls, standing at 4300 meters elevation. At last, this is Dana Monastery, finally in sight.

Dana Monastery has a very special heritage. In the year 1188, the monastery was changed into a Kargyu or White Sect, one of the Tibetan monastic sects. The founder of this monastery was Sangye Yerpa, thus the name of the sub-sect became Yerpa Kargyu. For 600 years prior to that, the monastery had

Nun with yogi / 尼姑與瑜珈修行者   Arriving Dana monastery / 抵達達那寺

寺廟。至今許多古物，包括兵器與盔甲，都保存在達那寺的藏品之中。

格薩爾王手下最英勇的將領與部會首長，總共有三十人。每人都有一座塔用來紀念他們。這些寶塔外形像古代的鐘，沿著海拔約 5000 公尺高的懸崖邊的兩個洞穴排列。雖然處在非常高的地方，但是每當霧氣散去時視野清晰，從達那寺仍可清楚看見。

果然，雲開霧散。一座彷彿被霧氣包覆的山峰漸漸露出來，隨著山上的霧氣逐漸散去，整排的寶塔便悠然地浮現眼前。

尼度尼瑪是達那寺的堪布。雖然正處於壯年，但是他處理這座古寺的日常事務已經很久了。他的仁波切兄弟把管理寺廟的責任都指派給他。現在寺裡有一百多位喇嘛，不過因為正值冬蟲夏草的採收季，很多人都回家去了。所以在我到訪期間只見到二十幾位喇嘛。不過清晨和傍晚仍聽得到鼓聲與誦經聲。

尼度告訴我有很多藏人都知道這間偏僻的寺廟，至於外國人或是出了中國以外的人士，幾乎沒人聽說過這間寺廟，更別說來達那寺拜訪了。他親自帶我去看兩座

been a Bon monastery, following the pre-Buddhist religion of Tibet. Thus, Dana is considered one of the oldest Tibetan monasteries, with a total of 1400 years of history.

Dana Monastery was designated a national protected cultural heritage site in 2006. Previously it was considered a provincially protected site. Today, one particular building, the highest on a protruded headland, is considered the oldest of the ensemble of buildings within the monastic compound.

For many Tibetan Buddhists, the Yerpa sub-sect, founded in the 12th Century within the Kargyu Sect, is believed to have merged with other sects, terminating its existence long ago. However, few know that the sub-sect survived in one lone monastery in a remote corner of the plateau. This has made Dana very special among the hundreds, and perhaps thousands, of monasteries throughout the Tibetan plateau, including those outside of China.

Furthermore, Dana is also known as the monastery of Ling. Gesar of Ling was a legendary king of the Kham region on the Tibetan plateau. He was born in Dengke, today's Dege, beside the Yangtze. His root guru was Sangye Yerpa, thus connecting him to Dana Monastery. Gesar's kingdom was known as Ling, where many battles were fought as Gesar unified the entire region, thus making him known as the most brilliant and courageous fighter throughout Tibetan history. Dana is the only monastery supposedly remaining among

Fog lifted / 霧散了

those that had Gesar's direct patronage. Today many relics, including battle weapons and armor, are preserved within the valued collection of Dana Monastery.

King Gesar's most gallant generals, or ministers of state, numbered thirty altogether. Each has a stupa (pagoda) dedicated to his memory. These white stupas, styled in ancient bell shape, are lined up in two grottoes along a precipitous cliff higher up the mountain, perhaps at 5,000 meters above sea level., Although perilously high, they can be seen from Dana monastery whenever the fog lifts and does not obliterate the view.

Sure enough, the sky clears a bit and the fog lifts. First a mountain peak reveals itself as if enveloped in mist. Then the hill where the stupas are located gradually clears and the lineup of pagodas come into full view.

Nidu Nyima is the abbot or Khempo of Dana Monastery. Though at the a prime age, he has been presiding over daily affairs of this ancient temple for some time. His brother is the Rinpoche who assigned all duties of managing the monastery to Nidu. Today there are over one hundred monks

Nidu the abbot / 尼度堪布

大殿，包括格薩爾寺，還有岬角上最古老的建築。這座
紅色建築是國家重點保護文化遺產的焦點。周圍裝了
二十四小時不歇息的監視器。

我的團隊獲准住在最古老的建築隔壁，就在稍微下面一
點的老屋裡。早晨和傍晚藏馬雞都唱著歌，有可能是春
天的求偶叫聲。然後，牠們走到我們住所那邊的山脊，
啄食地上喇嘛們灑給牠們的青稞顆粒。

早餐過後，我為中甸中心買了個誦經堂用的法鼓，之後
就啟程離開。山下有個具療效的溫泉。象鼻溫泉靠著一

attached to the monastery, but many are at home now during Cordyceps harvesting season. So there are only twenty some monks there during my visit. However, the sound of drums and chanting can still be heard early morning and into the evening.

Nidu tells me that his remote monastery is known to many Tibetans, but as far as foreigners or people outside of China are concerned, almost no one has heard of, let alone visited, Dana Monastery. He personally shows me the two Assembly Halls, including the Gesar Lhakang, as well as the oldest building on the headland. This building, in red color, is the focus of the national protected cultural site. Surveillance cameras are installed all around it for twenty-four hours monitoring the premises.

My team is allowed to stay in an old house adjacent and slightly below the oldest building. In the morning and evening, Tibetan Eared-pheasants sing their songs, probably mating calls for the spring. Soon after, they stroll to the ridge where we are staying, pecking on the ground for barley grains that the monks have scattered to feed them.

We take our leave after breakfast, after purchasing a monastic drum for the Buddhist prayer chapel at our Zhongdian Center. Down the hill is a wonderful medicinal hot spring. Elephant Nose Hot Spring formed with a natural mound now fully encrusted with white lime-like formations. At its foot are

座天然小丘，外層現在已經完全被硬化的白色石灰石物質包覆。小丘腳下有幾個自然形成的洞，每個都很適合一個人坐進去泡。因為時間匆促，我的腳只泡了差不多十分鐘就離開了。

車隊沿著來時的路線進入山區，我忍不住一直回望達那寺。它安坐在最美麗最壯觀的石灰岩山完美的搖籃裡。當然了，這時候我可以用字面上真正的意思，稱之為完美的「景觀」。

several naturally formed holes, each perfect for a person to sit inside and soak himself. As we are in a rush to leave, I barely get my feet in for a ten-minute treatment.

Driving off into the hills and retracing our tracks, I cannot help but keep looking back at Dana Monastery. It sits in a perfect cradle in the folds of the most beautiful and spectacular limestone hills. Surely, I can call this view a perfect "landscape," in the true sense of the word.

A perfect landscape / 完美的景觀

我的巴塘淵源

MY BATANG CONNECTION

Batang, Sichuan – August 1, 2017

我的巴塘淵源

西藏共產黨與基督教的搖籃

平措有兩件武器：一個像康巴寶劍般銳利，是他的堅毅不屈；另一個老練又內斂，是馬克思辯證唯物論。這兩件武器讓他成為倖存者而非殉道者。在他所謂的「秦城黨校」熬過了 18 年單獨監禁，那是北京郊外的最高戒備監獄，專門囚禁最該死或最無辜的中國高幹與精英知識分子。平措的身高跟智慧都很高。他的獄友，雖然他們從未謀面，都是像四人幫，聲名狼藉的政治異議者。進秦城監獄的都是特殊人物，如果能活著出來就更傳奇了。

1988 年我在平措的出生地巴塘初次認識他。平措汪傑（大多數人叫他平汪）生於 1922 年一月，出生在青藏高原東部的西康。我認識他時，他已經是 66 歲的老人了，出獄十年，重新成為中國人民代表大會裡的高官。我比他小了快四分之一世紀，那時我是剛離開美國國家地理雜誌的熱血記者，特別熱愛中國少數民族，尤其是生活在青藏高原上的那些。

MY BATANG CONNECTION

Cradle of Tibetan Communist Party and Christianity

Phuntso had two weapons: one sharp like a Khampa sword, his stubborn perseverance, the other seasoned and well-tempered, Marxist dialectical materialism. Those two qualities made him a survivalist rather than a martyr, living through 18 years of solitary confinement in what he called the "Qincheng Party School," a maximum security prison outside of Beijing reserved for the most deserving, or underserving, high cadres and intellectual elites of China. Phuntso was both, in height and in intellect. His cellmates, though they never saw or ran into each other, were the likes of the Gang of Four and notorious political dissidents. Anyone who got into Qingcheng was someone special, and even more so if they got out alive.

I first met Phuntso in Batang, the town of his birth, in 1988. Phuntso Wangye (most call him PhunWang) was born in January 1922 in what is known as Kham in the eastern part of the Tibetan plateau. By the time I met him, he was an ageing man of 66, out of prison already for ten years and reinstated as a high official within the People's Congress of the PRC. I was almost a quarter century his junior, fresh out of the National Geographic as a budding

Phuntso (front middle) before imprisoned / 入獄前的平措（第一排中間）

平措出獄恢復職位之後第一次回家時，巴塘鎮歡欣鼓
舞——並不是因為他低調地造訪，而是為期一週的慶
典剛剛開始。陪伴他的是我的好友之一，也是巴塘出
身的札西慈仁。

「好人不抽菸，壞人不喝酒，」是札西的口頭禪，也
是讓他不抽菸的原則。札西是一位西藏學術團體領
袖，曾帶著五人學者團在 1988 年受探險學會之邀訪
問美國。1950 年代中期身為青年幹部的他，曾經陪同
來自西方的記者團從四川沿剛建成的公路進入西藏到
拉薩。

Phuntso (front middle) after release / 出獄後的平措（第一排中間）

journalist turned enthusiast of Chinese minorities, especially those living on the Tibetan plateau.

Phuntso was going home for the first time after he was released and reinstated. Batang town was jubilant - not because of his low-key visit, but because a week-long festival was just starting. He was accompanied by a close friend of mine, Tashi Tsering, who also hailed from Batang.

"Good man doesn't smoke and bad man doesn't drink," was Tashi's favorite quote, which upheld his abstention from smoking. Tashi was leader of the first Tibetan academic group of five scholars to visit the US at the invitation

札西告訴我那八位記者被要求進入高原之前作體檢的故事。沒有人能壓抑高昂的興奮感而通過血壓必須低於130的標準。可憐的醫師叫他們先回飯店，冷靜下來，隔天再回來，希望札西能成功地把這八個人的血壓平均值降到130以下！團體的隨從中有位正在崛起的中國年輕外交官，馬毓真。我在洛杉磯初次認識馬，後來他當上了中國駐英大使。

我在巴塘跟平措與札西一起，觀賞了西藏歌劇，在舉行典禮的大帳篷裡喝酥油茶，隨著聞名的巴塘弦子（一種像小提琴的二弦樂器）跳舞，甚至跟兩個探險學會同僚參加了晚間表演，畢尉林博士和仁米山，邊唱美國歌邊跳舞。整個過程，平措都穿著他的藏服，卡其色垂到腳踝的長袍。

第三天，藏人鬥毆，一位剛從大學畢業的年輕人因此喪命。在武功和雄性氣概被襃揚而非抑制的地方這似乎很正常。我曾經聽過某位巴塘出身的西藏代表說過，這位代表曾經在國民黨政府部會級的「台灣蒙藏委員會」工作過。「在我們家鄉，如果與人打鬥負傷回家，家人會先檢查你的傷勢是在正面或背面。若是正面，他們會好好照顧你。若在背後，他們可能會猶豫甚至不理你，猜想你一定是轉身逃跑了。」這就是當地對康巴男人英勇

of CERS in 1988. As a young cadre in the mid-1950s, he escorted a corps of journalists from the West and entered Tibet to Lhasa by road from Sichuan.

Tashi told me a story of eight journalists being asked to undergo a physical before entering the plateau. None could contain their excitement to pass the test requiring their blood pressure to be under 130. The poor doctor asked them to get back to their hotel, calm down, and return the following day, hoping he could manage to draw an average among the eight for a count below 130! Among escorts to that group was another young, up and coming Chinese diplomat, Ma Yuzhen. I first met Ma in Los Angeles and he would later become the Ambassador to the UK from China.

At Batang together with Phuntso and Tashi, we attended Tibetan opera, drank buttered tea in a huge ceremonial tent, danced to the famous Batang xuanzi (a two-stringed, fiddle-like instrument) and even joined an evening performance during which two of my CERS colleagues, Dr. Bleisch and Ahrin Mishan, performed an Americana song and dance number. Through it all, Phuntso sported his Tibetan costume, an ankle-length robe in Khaki color.

On the third day, a brawl among some feuding Tibetans broke out and a recent college graduate was killed. That seemed quite normal in a region where martial prowess and manly behavior were glorified rather than curtailed. I remember hearing from a Tibetan delegate, originally from Batang, at Taiwan's

氣概的標準。

為何平措即使坐了這麼久的牢，還是這麼受尊重？他在
14 歲離家到南京受教育，所以藏語和漢語都很流利。
在學校，他迷上閱讀激進的書刊，當時主要是馬克思和
列寧的著作。1939 年他 17 歲時，在重慶的藏人學生中
創立了西藏共產黨，之後很快把他們的小團體擴張到重
要的德格、巴塘與拉薩。幾年後，他們的地下黨員遍佈
了喀木、西藏和雲南。在他巴塘家裡的四兄弟中，1949
年之前已經有三位加入了共產黨的游擊隊了。

毛澤東的紅軍贏得內戰建立中華人民共和國之後，他的西
藏黨被中共吸收。平措成為後來北京和拉薩間談判與擬
定和平協議的主力。他不只在西藏的新政府很活躍，也是
毛主席跟達賴喇嘛、班禪喇嘛幾次重要會議中的翻譯。

透過他在西藏共產黨內的人脈和指導，許多巴塘年輕人
成為西藏的第一代高官。西藏自治區前任副書記丹增告
訴我，第一代的西藏幹部高達 80% 是巴塘人，甚至自
治區的最高機構裡有 60% 是巴塘出身的。

這當然是平措早期從事地下運動的貢獻。甚至在平措人
生最後幾年（他死於 2014 年），他成為馬克思主義的

Mongolian and Tibetan Affairs Commission, a ministry level office within the Nationalist government. "In our hometown, if there is a fight and you come home wounded, the family would first check to see if your injury is inflicted on the front or on the back. If it is front, they'll take good care of you. If the wound is on your back, they would hesitate and may ignore you, assuming that you must have turned and run away." Such were the expectations of bravery attached to the Khampa men in the region.

Why was Phuntso so highly regarded, even after a long prison term? He left home at 14 and was educated in Nanjing, thus was fluent in both Tibetan and Chinese. While at school, he was attracted to reading progressive books and journals, at the time mainly writings of Marx and Lenin. In 1939, at age 17, he founded the Tibetan Communist Party among Tibetan students then

Phuntso with Mao, Dalai & Panchen Lamas / 平措與毛澤東、達賴、班禪喇嘛合影

理論家與哲學家，這些都歸功於在獄中長期獨處自學，因為唯一能夠閱讀的書都是馬克思主義。

但是巴塘在平措出生之前就已經是教育重鎮了。我的朋友格桑群佩（洋名卡森）就是個例子，他就是 1908 年美國傳教士艾伯特 • 薛爾頓博士創辦學校的受惠者。格桑也是出身自薛爾頓博士創立的巴塘孤兒院。戰爭期間，格桑被派到美國學飛行，先是當上戰鬥機飛行員然後當上轟炸機機長。無疑的他是第一位藏人飛行員。

1989 年我在台灣演講時初次認識格桑。當時，演講內容包含許多我在那個時期的西藏探險經歷。我走進演講廳後很驚訝地發現裡面坐滿了穿制服的軍官。我的東道主也是好友蔣彥士博士是當時台灣總統府秘書長。是蔣彥士介紹李登輝給蔣介石之子蔣經國。後來李登輝成為台灣總統。蔣博士邀請了三軍軍官來聽我的演講，了解難得的中國西藏第一手資訊。

當時格桑以蒙藏委員會主委的身分帶著夫人一起出席，但夫人僅僅穿著一般服飾。夫人吳香蘭（藏名伊西娜珍）是國民黨多任期的國大代表。

聽出我演講內容對西藏有深切的認識後，格桑跟我很

in Chongqing, and soon after expanded their small but crucial recruit to Dege,
Batang, and then Lhasa. Over the years, their underground members covered
Kham, Tibet and Yunnan. Of four boys in his family from Batang, three be-
came Communist guerilla fighters before 1949.

His Tibetan Party was absorbed into the Chinese Communist Party when
Mao's Red Army won the civil war and founded the PRC. Phuntso became a
major force in the subsequent negotiation and drafting of agreements between
Beijing and Lhasa. He was not only active within the new government in
Tibet, but acted as interpreter for Chairman Mao during several important
meetings between the Chairman and the Dalai and Panchen Lamas.

Through his connection and mentoring within the Tibetan Communist Par-
ty, many young Batang men became the first generation of high officials in
Tibet. As told to me by the former Vice-party Secretary of TAR, up to 80%
of first generation Tibetan cadres of the PRC were from Batang, and per-
haps as many as 60% within the Autonomous Region's highest office were of
Batang origin.

This was certainly a contribution from the early recruitment by Phuntso when
he was setting up his underground movement. Even during the final years of
Phuntso's life (he died in 2014), he became a Marxist ideologue and philos-
opher, which he attributed to years of self study during his long isolation in

Dr Hardy pointing at his house / 哈迪博士指著他家房子

快變成朋友，雖然他的火爆脾氣是出了名的。格桑夫
人出身木里，是前任木里國王的表親，1949 年之前在
康定的學校任教。那幾年每次我去台北，我們都聊得
很開心。他向我透露他在印度西藏邊界附近進行過幾
次比較危險的任務，讓印度情報單位總是想要掌握他
的行蹤。

我認識格桑時，他仍然定期會去鳳凰城參加飛行中隊
的聚會。後來格桑來洛杉磯的時候曾住在我家，他有
兩個兒子，我見過一位，兩位都是受英國教育的心臟
科醫師，在加拿大多倫多行醫。孩子們持續了巴塘重視

prison when the only available reading was Marxist books.

But Batang had been an education center even before Phuntso was born. My friend Kesang Chompel (Carson) is one example, a beneficiary of a school started in 1908 by Dr. Albert Shelton, an American missionary. Kesang came out of the Batang orphanage, also founded by Dr. Shelton. During the War, Kesang was sent to America to learn flying, first becoming a fighter pilot and later captaining a bomber. There is little doubt that he was the first Tibetan aviator.

I met Kesang at my first lecture delivered in Taiwan in 1989. At the time, the lecture covered much of my exploration of Tibet up to that point. I was surprised as I entered the lecture room that it was filled with military officers in uniform. Dr. Tsiang Yen-si, my host and close friend, was secretary general of the President of Taiwan at the time. It was Tsiang, introduced Lee Teng-hui to Chiang Ching-kuo, son of Chiang Kai-shek. Lee subsequently became the President of Taiwan. For my lecture, Dr. Tsiang had invited officers from all three forces to hear a rare talk on China's Tibetan frontier.

Kesang was with his wife in civilian clothes. He came representing his office/ ministry, being a commissioner of the Mongolian Tibetan Affairs Commission. His wife, Wu Xianglan (Yeshi Lhadon in Tibetan), was a long-time member of the Congress of the Kuomintang.

教育的傳統。

或許我與巴塘最特殊的淵源是在美國的巴塘俱樂部，會員來自薛爾頓、奧格頓、哈迪、洛夫提、麥克勞、鄧肯等家族。威廉（比爾）·哈迪博士讀到我在美國國家地理雜誌描述西藏地區旅程的報導後寫信給我。那年是1986年，我剛創辦了探險學會。

哈迪1916年出生於巴塘的傳教士家庭，1926年十歲時離開。他一輩子都希望有一天能回到出生地看看。透過通信交流，我後來也去了田納西州橡樹嶺見他，我們決定帶他回巴塘，在當時要幫外國人申請許可是很困難的。但是透過我的友人札西慈仁，我們成功地取得許可證，包括隨行照顧他的兒子小威廉，哈迪雖是小兒科醫師，但是畢竟也70歲了，身體並沒有那麼硬朗。

說起1987年他的返鄉之旅，當時我開著探險學會唯一的一部越野車，路途對那個年紀的人是很辛苦的，因為那時還沒有柏油路通往巴塘。從我們簡陋的昆明基地出發，花了將近一個星期才到巴塘。哈迪博士帶了他的家族相簿，靠黑白老照片尋找他的故居，並且也一路比較過去與現在。

Through my lecture he heard my intimate knowledge on Tibet, Kesang and I became fast friends, though his hot temper with others was notorious. His wife came from Muli, a cousin of the former King of Muli, and had taught school in Kanding before 1949. We had many lively discussions whenever I visited Taipei during those years. He revealed to me some of the more hazardous operations he conducted near the border of India with Tibet and how the Indian intelligence service was always trying to determine his whereabouts.

When I met Kesang, he still went regularly to gatherings in Phoenix for his squadron's reunion. When later Kesang visited and stayed with me at my home in Los Angeles, I met one of his two sons, both cardiologists educated in the UK and by then practicing in Toronto Canada. The children had maintained the fine education tradition of Batang.

Perhaps my most unusual Batang connection was the Batang Club in America, with members from the families of the Sheltons, Ogdens, Hardys, Loftis's, MacLeods, Duncans, etc. Dr. William (Bill) Hardy first wrote me upon reading my story in the National Geographic, describing my travels through the Tibetan region. It was at a time when I had just started CERS in 1986.

Hardy was born in Batang to a missionary family in 1916 and left in 1926

我們受到對口政府官員與部門的接待。走訪了哈迪博士出生的故居，美國傳教團曾經為病人進口病床的舊醫院舊址。病床已經移到康定的州立醫院去了。哈迪博士指著河邊的一塊大石頭告訴我，以前就在這裡處決罪犯，不管是民事上的或是政治犯。

我們去了城外的甲坡頂，一座寬廣的花園坐落在傳教團醫院和學校的舊址。傳教士帶來的蘋果樹在此依舊開花結果。這座果園可以採收到出名的玫瑰香蘋果。我們到的時候剛好趕上品嚐這種美味的紅色小蘋果。到訪之後兩年，一場 6.7 級大地震震翻了蘋果樹，還有許多建築物。

回到洛杉磯家之後，我去拜訪桃樂絲 · 薛爾頓，她是 1908 年創立巴塘教會的艾伯特 · 薛爾頓博士的女兒。

Tashi with delegation to US in 1988 / 1988 年札西與赴美代表團

when he was ten years old. All his life, he had hoped to return one day to the town of his birth. Through communications and later a visit to meet him at Oakridge Tennessee, we decided to take him back to Batang, a very difficult trip to get permission for at that time for a foreigner. But somehow through Tashi Tseren my friend, we managed to get the required permissions, including for his son William Jr., who came along to escort his father Dr. Hardy, though a pediatrics doctor, was 70 years old and quite frail.

His return trip in 1987, with me driving CERS's single car at the time, was rough going for a man of his age. This was long before the road to Batang was paved. Starting from our humble base in Kunming, it took almost a week of driving to reach Batang. Dr. Hardy brought along his family album with old black and white pictures to seek out his old haunts, as well as to compare the past to the present.

We were well received by respective government officials and departments. We visited the house of Dr. Hardy's birth, the old hospital ground where the American missionary had imported beds for patients. These had since been moved to the prefecture hospital in Kanding. Dr. Hardy showed me a huge rock by the river where, he said, execution of criminals, civil or political, used to take place.

We visited Japoding, an extensive garden right outside of town, where the old

Phuntso in Tibet in the 1950s / 1950 年代平措攝於西藏

薛爾頓一家在巴塘住了很多年,直到 1922 年薛爾頓博士在前往西藏的途中被殺害。那時,桃樂絲和妹妹才剛上加州的寄宿學校,母親芙蘿拉則是在印度。現在紐華克博物館豐富的西藏文物收藏就是薛爾頓博士在某次放長假時帶回美國的。

我在桃樂絲位於波莫納的退休傳教士之家,翻閱了他們在中國時期的老照片,特別是在巴塘的那些年。我感到很榮幸他們讓我成為巴塘俱樂部極少數的會員之一。有一次平措的兒子從紐約打電話給我,向我詢問會

mission hospital and school once stood. Here is where the apple trees brought by the missionaries still bloomed and bore fruit. The famous Mei Gui Xiang (Rose Fragrance) apples were harvested from this orchard. We were just in time to taste these small, delicious, reddish apples. Two years after our visit, a major 6.7 earthquake would rock the apples, as well as many of the buildings, to their bases.

Back home in Los Angeles, I visited Dorothy Shelton, daughter of Dr. Albert Shelton who founded the Batang mission in 1908. The Shelton's spent long years in Batang, until 1922 when Dr. Shelton was murdered on his way into Tibet. At that time, Dorothy and her sister had just started boarding school in California while Flora, the mother, was in India. The Newark Museum now holds a large collection of Tibetan artefacts brought back to the United States by Dr. Shelton during one of his furloughs.

At Dorothy's retirement home for missionaries in Pomona, I thumbed through old pictures about their time in China, in particular their years in Batang. I felt honored that they had included me in their short list of members of their own Batang Club. Once Phuntso's son called me from New York, requesting the list so he could contact the "Batang Gang" in America. I gladly obliged and sent it to him.

Now I am again back in Batang, after perhaps a dozen trips here over the

員名單以便可以聯絡在美國的「巴塘幫」，我欣然同意將名單寄給他。

這些年來跑了巴塘十幾次，如今我又回到這裡。我重訪在舊原址上剛剛重建完成的傳教士醫院。旁邊有個舊招牌：「華西醫院」——證明這裡曾經是教會醫院。這裡的一切跟我卅年前看到的已經完全不同了。

我從一座河橋進入南門，這裡曾經有城牆圍繞整個舊城區防禦軍隊入侵，無論來自東邊的中國中央王朝，或西邊的拉薩。巴塘像三明治夾在中間，半獨立，時而效忠中國時而依附西藏。

從南門橋經過兩間房子後轉進一條五米小巷，那裡就是平措的老家。我敲門進去，要找他的么弟洛桑汪嘉。他剛好出門了，但是孫子說他過幾分鐘就會回來。不到十分鐘，有位老人走進門。他很矮，不像平措高大的體格。洛桑聽說我是跟他哥哥來過巴塘的人，便開心地露出微笑。

現在，院子裡有兩棟藏族風格的房屋，舊的那棟有著傳統巴塘建築的紅磚牆，另一棟則被刷得很白很新。趁著洛桑的孫女正忙著幫我們準備巴塘出名的手工麵時，

years. I revisited the missionary hospital, which had just been totally rebuilt on its original ground. An old sign on the floor - "West China Hospital" - gave evidence to the site being once the grounds of the mission hospital. No other scene resembles what I had seen thirty years ago in the slightest.

I crossed the river bridge and entered the South Gate, once connected to a wall surrounding the entire old town to guard against intruding armies, be they from the east from the Central Chinese court, or from the west from Lhasa. Batang was very much sandwiched in the middle, semi-independent, yet at times pledging allegiance to either China or Tibet.

Two houses down from the South Gate bridge and inside a five-meter alley is Phuntso's old home. I knocked on the door and entered, asking to visit Lobsang Wangyal, his youngest brother. He was momentarily out, but the grandchildren said he would return in a few minutes. Not quite ten minutes later, an old man came through the door. He was rather short, unlike Phuntso's tall stature. But Lobsang was ready with a big smile, hearing that I was the person who had visited Batang before with his brother.

Today, the courtyard premises have two Tibetan style houses, one old and sporting the traditional reddish adobe wall color of Batang buildings, the other almost brand new and white-washed. While Lobsang's granddaughters were busy preparing the famous Batang hand-made noodles for us, he showed me

洛桑帶我參觀新屋。「這棟房子是蓋在我們老家舊屋的原址上，平措很想把它改裝成博物館，紀念西藏共產黨的歷史和功績。」洛桑告訴我。

「大家都說好了，建造費用由我們所有兄弟分攤，」洛桑又說，「但現在不可能了，因為有些敏感問題。」他遺憾地嘆道。樓上的牆上有一幅平措與洛桑父親的畫像。

不久我們回到戶外的庭院，邊喝茶邊吃麵，那麵好吃地讓我一碗接一碗。洛桑又拿出他的家族相簿來，我對其中的一些照片非常感興趣，包括平措與家人早期的黑白照與手繪彩色照；以及 1950 年代初期他跟毛主席、周恩來、達賴與班禪喇嘛的合照。

另一本相簿裡是平措在北京葬禮的照片。送花的人有習近平，胡錦濤，幾乎所有政府的高官都有。還有些照片是出席葬禮的高幹，包括當任許久的西藏黨委書記陰法唐。

洛桑告訴我他聽說西藏學者高史坦（Mel Goldstein）寫了他哥哥的傳記，最近在香港也出了中文版。他很想要一本，說他只會看中文不會藏文。他在解放後的新

the new house. "This house is built on the ground of our old family house, and Phuntso very much wanted to turn it into a museum, a place to honor the history and heritage of the Tibetan Communist Party," Lobsang said to me.

"This was agreed upon and expenses of the construction were to be shared by all our siblings," Lobsang added. "Now it is no longer possible, as there are some sensitivity issues," he lamented with a tone of regret. Upstairs along the wall was a drawing of Phuntso and Lobsang's father.
Soon we were back out in the garden, having tea as the delicious noodles were served, one small bowl after another. Lobsang brought out his family album. I was most interested in the early black and whites and some hand-painted color photos of Phuntso and his family, as well as those taken in the early 1950s with Chairman Mao, Zhou En-lai, the Dalai Lama and the Panchen Lama.

Another album was filled with pictures of Phuntso's funeral in Beijing. Among those who sent flowers were Xi Jinping, Hu Jintao, and in fact almost all senior officials in government. There were also pictures showing high cadres who attended the funeral, including long-time Tibet Party Secretary Yin Fatong.

Lobsang told me that he had heard of a biography about his brother, authored by Tibetan scholar Mel Goldstein, and that the book had also been recently published in Chinese in Hong Kong. He was very eager to get a copy, telling

政權下受教育，當小學校長直到幾年前才退休，現在他 78 歲了。與他道別的時候我答應回香港之後會帶一本給他。

漫步走回附近的甲坡頂，我從蘋果樹摘了幾顆半紅的蘋果。附近的女士說蘋果已經熟了可以吃了。我咬了一口，滋味苦甜參半，不像從前那樣好吃。我回想巴塘這些與我巧遇的風雲人物，現在他們都走了，只留下各自有趣的故事和歷史，就像現在的巴塘蘋果一樣苦中帶甜。

Phuntso with son and family / 平措抱兒子與家人

me that he only read Chinese and not Tibetan. He was educated under the new regime after liberation and had been an elementary school master until retirement some years ago. Today, he is 78 years of age. I promised that I would get a copy of the book to him after I return to Hong Kong as I bade him farewell.

Strolling back to nearby Japoding, I picked from an apple tree a few half red apples. The lady in a nearby house said they were ripe and ready. I took a bite and it was bitter sweet, unlike the old days when they were most palatable. I thought of all these fascinating people of Batang who had crossed paths with my life. Now they are all gone. What is left is each of their interesting stories and histories, bitter sweet just like the Batang apples of today.

Young cadre Phuntso /
年輕幹部時期的平措

Phuntso between Dalai & Panchen /
平措坐在達賴和班禪中間

回憶鄧永鏘爵士 REMEMBERING SIR DAVID TANG

CX885 LA to HK – September 20/21, 2017

EMIGRATION.

CUBA COMMISSION.

Unison

SERIES

For Howman,

The only real China explorer of our age,

David Tang

DAVID TANG'S
has deteriorated
aimed to elevate
become a bore
readers otherw
more genuine
taken construc
One who cann
time with syco

If you think th
social standing
famous and a
and commanc
lar contribute
paper in the
established c

回憶鄧永鏘爵士

鄧永鏘〈Sir David Tang〉幾年前在他的書中寫道「我想，人有一天終究都會躺在棺材裡。在這裡我想要建議我的親朋好友。當有一天我躺在棺材裡，你們可能會來看我。我不想要聽到你們低語說『他有個好心腸，總是幫助慈善機構，當志工，幫助他人』。我只想要聽到你驚訝地說『等一下，他剛剛好像動了一下』。」

飛機從洛杉磯起飛，在飛行了 15 個小時之後，於晚間 7 點抵達香港。每位乘客都有一夜好眠，除了一個人之外，一個正在寫兩篇文章和一篇新聞通訊的人。

當我寫完這篇關於 David 的文章後，我從座位 26G 起身拿行李。猜猜誰就坐在我正前方 25G 的座位？正是 David 的妹妹 Alice Tang。就在六週前 8 月 12 日那天，我在《中國會》和她首次見了一面，那個午餐是臨時的，一如往常都是由 David 幫我安排的。Alice 是 Vivienne Tam 的朋友，而 Vivienne 是我的客人。

CX885 LA to HK – September 20 / 21, 2017

REMEMBERING SIR DAVID TANG

Written some years ago by David Tang in his book, "I think a man someday must lay in a coffin. Here I would like to advice my relatives and friends. One day when I have to be laid inside a coffin, each of you may come and see me. I don't want to hear you whispering, 'he has a kind heart, always giving to charity and volunteering, warmly helping others'. I only want to hear that one of you would say in shock, 'Wait, looks like he just made a move'.

As our plane landed in Hong Kong 7pm in the evening after a 15 hours flight, every passenger had a good sleep on the long flight from Los Angeles except one, who had been working on two articles and a newsletter.

After I finished this piece about David Tang, I rose from seat 26G to remove my luggage from above. And who was sitting directly one seat in front of me in 25G? David Tang's sister Alice Tang. I had met her briefly for the first time less than six weeks ago on August 12 at the China Club during a last minute arranged lunch, for which David, like always, had helped secure my reservations. She was a friend of Vivienne Tam, whom I was hosting.

4 月 28 日，*David* 給我一封電子郵件關於另外一個派對：
意外發現的美好！
晚餐你們會有幾位參加？你希望幾點開始？

Sir David Tang

真的是意外的發現。不過我想一定是鄧永鏘爵士的安排，我原本的班機被取消了，剛剛好讓我跟他的妹妹可以搭上同一班飛機，座位一定也是他安排的。

我的摯友鄧永鏘爵士於 8 月 30 日辭世，我一直想要寫一篇文章紀念他。拖了近一個月，許多思緒在腦中，直到我的班機 *CX897* 被取消。我被困在 *LAX* 機場 7 個小時，然後再轉搭下一班飛機 *CX885*，飛行 15 個小時後回香港。

既然 *David* 喜歡在週末的《金融時報》專欄裡寫些跟飛行有關的文章，我想我在飛機上也來寫一篇是挺合適的。像他一樣，我有幸搭乘過多次私人飛機，和他一樣，我搭的也不是我自己的飛機。不過今天我搭的是商務艙，這艙等對 *David* 來說還算是勉強可以，對探險家來說可是相當的豪華。

On April 28, David had written in an email to me about another party:

Wonderful serendipity!

How many of you in the party for the dinner? What time you would like it to start?

Sir David Tang

Serendipity indeed. But I rather like to think that Sir David had arranged the canceled flight that put me on the same flight with his sister, and the seating. I have wanted to write a tribute to Sir David Tang, my good friend who passed away on August 30. But I procrastinated for almost a month, as many thoughts came to mind, until my flight CX897 from Los Angeles to Hong Kong was canceled. I was stuck at LAX for seven hours before boarding the next flight CX885 for a 15 hours flight home.

Since David often liked to write about flying in his column in the Weekend Financial Times, I thought it appropriate to finally write my piece in flight. Like him, I had the pleasure of flying private, and like him, it was not my jet. But today, I'm in Business Class, minimum comfort for David, but adequate luxury for an explorer.

On further thinking, I find it best to select below some correspondence we ex-

My father against Ping Pong machine / 我的父親與乒乓球機對打

我想了想，覺得選一些過去一年來他跟我的通信是最適合不過的。如此的話，這些文字都是直接出自於他本人，而不是經過我的描述。

Sir David's Tang 的書信以加底線呈現。

2 Jun 2017, 06:55, How Man ‹hmwong@cers.org.hk› 寫：

Hi David,

我才剛從西藏回來，再過一週就要去巴拉望。因為這些衛星影像的關係，報告現在還有點複雜，不過應該過幾天就會好了⋯⋯這是第 5 個我們去到而且定位的河流源頭⋯⋯等了 3 年，中間斷斷續續，不過並不想讓別人知道，就怕萬一我們到不了⋯⋯不像其他人還沒出發前就開記者會等等⋯⋯*HM*

〈伊洛瓦底江源頭 *.docx*〉

changed over the last year. This way, the words come directly from him, rather than as depicted by me. Sir David's writings are underlined.

On 2 Jun 2017, at 06:55, How Man <hmwong@cers.org.hk> wrote:

Hi David,

Just back from Tibet, leaving in a week for Palawan. Report is a bit complicated with all the satellite images so should be ready in a few days....This is the fifth source we defined and reached....been waiting for three years working on it on and off, but didn't want to make any noise in case we cannot reach it....unlike many others who gave press conference etc before embarking on expedition....HM

<Irrawaddy Source Release.docx>

From: Sir David Tang [mailto:dt@dwctang.com]

Sent: Friday, 2 June 2017 7:14 AM

To: How Man <hmwong@cers.org.hk>

Subject: Re: Irrawaddy Source reached....

You lead an amazing life!

How can I get another couple of those ping pong machines?

Sir David Tang

From: Sir David Tang [mailto:dt@dwctang.com]

Sent: Friday, 2 June 2017 7:14 AM

To: How Man <hmwong@cers.org.hk>

Subject: Re: 抵達伊洛瓦底江的源頭

你過得真是多采多姿！

我怎樣才可以再取得幾台那個乒乓球機？

Sir David Tang

6 Jun 2017, 08:37, <hmwong@cers.org.hk> 寫：

Hi David,

我們之前的型號 E 還是最好的，不要買最新的型號 G，除非你是奧運級的球手。

HM

我追求是伊卡洛斯！ *Sir David Tang*

（附錄：古希臘伊卡洛斯欲飛行，但過近太陽而折翅）

David 和我同屬於互相崇拜協會〈*Mutual Admiration Society*〉。他的 *email* 變得越來越短，在他去世前不到 3 個月。儘管如此，這就是 *David*。雖然捕捉不到 *David* 的樣貌，但確實地捕捉到 *David* 的精神，他去訂了幾台最新型的乒乓球機。

Bird musical notes / 樂譜上的小鳥

On 6 Jun 2017, at 08:37, <hmwong@cers.org.hk> wrote:

Hi David, Our former model E remains the best, so don't order the latest G model unless you are Olympiad grade. HM

I am Icarus in ambition! Sir David Tang

David and I must belong to the Mutual Admiration Society. His emails became briefer and briefer, as they happened less than three months before he passed away. Nonetheless, it epitomizes that spirit which is so very David. Quite to form for David, perhaps not in physical form but certainly in spirit,

幾年前 David 來探險學會石澳的展覽館，之後去鶴咀參
觀我的攝影工作室。他看到我對著乒乓發球機打球，馬
上就訂了 5 台。太了解 David 了，他應該在每一個家都
會擺一台，剩下的可能就送給朋友。

看到我的鋼琴，那是可以自彈的鋼琴，他大方地坐下
來演奏，彈得很好很有感情。他彈得即興獨奏少了幾
個音節──他沒有完成的演奏 *(http://cacaoworkshop.
com:5000/sharing/RZAWqWlhZ)*。我的鋼琴上面有一張黑
白照，幾隻鳥停在五條電線上。那是在緬甸拍的，象徵
樂譜的照片。*David* 轉身過來問我，「你想要聽牠們的
聲音嗎？」他於是開始彈奏，把那張照片的樂譜彈奏出
來，這就是 *David*。

幾天後，*13 Jun 2017, 05:04, How Man <hmwong@cers.org.
hk>* 寫：
Hi David,
我在巴拉望，剛從巴塔人手中收到一隻小野豬，還不到
兩個月。另外有一隻一個月大的八哥，還不會說話，但
是他們說餵牠吃辣椒牠就會講話，有可能是因為太辣了
牠一定要叫出來！附上兩篇文章，一篇是我寫的伊洛瓦
底江源頭報告。另外一篇關於古巴，由 *CERS* 夥伴劉教

he went ahead and ordered a couple of the latest, high-powered machines.

A few years ago, David came to our Shek O Exhibit House, followed by a visit to my photo studio at Cape D'Aguilar. He saw me playing against the Ping Pong serving machine, and immediately ordered his first batch of five. Knowing David, probably one for each of his homes, and may be the remaining ones for friends.

Seeing my piano, which also can self-play, he sat down and hit the keys with great skill and enthusiasm. He finished this impromptu recital short of the last few bars - his Unfinished Melody. http://cacaoworkshop.com:5000/ sharing/RZAWqWlhZ On my piano was a framed picture in black and white, of birds sitting on five electric wires. It was taken in Myanmar, symbolizing musical notes. True to form again, he turned and asked, "You want to hear what that sounds like?" and proceeded to play out the picture as if they were real musical notes.

Several days later, **on 13 Jun 2017, at 05:04, How Man <hmwong@cers.org. hk> wrote:**
Hi David, Now in Palawan, just received from the Batak people we work on a baby boar, barely two months, and a month-old mynah, not yet talking but they said I should feed it chili then it will talk, probably too spicy thus it has to

DT greeting Ho Chiu-lan / David 歡迎何秋蘭女士

授提供，他兩年前從堪薩斯大學退休。我會再另外寄給
你。祝好，HM。

你的生活好純真！ *Sir David Tang*

他的回覆很簡短，我們之間的通信追溯到 5 年前，有
3 次是 David 以古巴榮譽領事的身分幫我拿到古巴的簽
證。我去古巴目的是拍紀錄片。還記得那次我去 David
在半山的家，那時他躺在床上對他的「聽眾」抱怨健康
狀況，而我則是坐著享用我的早餐。他將我的簽證日期
空白，讓我自己填。當我起身離開時，他給了我一盒雪
茄，但是少了一支。

在哈瓦那，我們訪談兩位年長的女士，兩位曾經是粵劇

cry out! Attached are two pieces of article, one is my report on the Irrawaddy source ..... The other piece on Cuba is supported by CERS for our associate Prof Lau who retired from the Univ. of Kansas two years ago. I will forward that separately. Best, HM

What a pure life you lead! Sir David Tang

His answer was brief, but this exchange hails back to five years before when, for three times, I obtained my Cuban visa from David in his role as Honorary Counsel to Cuba. I was going to Havana for the making of a documentary film. The visas weren't acquired at his office, nor by mail. Each time I met David at his home in Mid-level, just a bit below the Peak Tram station on May Road. On one of those occasions, he gave his "audience" in bed while I sat and enjoyed breakfast, as he lamented now and then about his physical condition. He would leave the dates on the visa open, for me to fill in as I wished. As I rose to leave, he gave me a box of cigar, opened but with only one cigar missing.

In Havana, we interviewed two elderly, Cuban ladies who were once Cantonese opera performers. Ho Chiu-lan, despite being full Cuban born, became a lead in Cantonese opera in Cuba, because she was adopted by a Chinese immigrant as his step-daughter when she was three years old. David generously offered to pay for passage for both of the ladies to Hong Kong from Cuba, and

的演員。何秋蘭，即使是個純正的古巴人，卻能在古巴的粵劇界裡擔當主角，因為她的養父是從中國來的移民，在她 3 歲的時候收養她。*David* 很慷慨地出錢邀請這兩位女士從古巴前來香港，他也親自來石澳觀賞她們的粵劇表演。當然，這兩位女士後來也到我們石澳的展覽館做演出。

過去一年 *David* 寄來的電子郵件一部分反應出他心理和身體的狀態，還有他與書籍的關係。

4 Apr, 2017, 12:20 pm, Sir David Tang <dt@dwctang.com> 寫：
- 我不確定我有另外一本古巴書！事實上我確定我只有一本。你千萬千萬千萬不要把重要的書借給別人！我從來都不借！
- 你再也找不到這本書了。我有原始版，複製了 10 本給你還有其他人。它很負面因為每個中國人都在抱怨！每一位！
- 18 號但是我 21 號又要離開！二月一號回。
我買了一本你寫有關西藏的書送給皮帕・米德爾頓，王子的弟婦！

30 Dec 2016, 12:05, How Man <hmwong@cers.org.hk> 在日本寫：

attended Cantonese opera performance together with them in Shek O. The two ladies went on to perform at our Shek O house later.

Random emails from David over the last year reflected in part his state of mind and physical conditions, and his relationship to books.

On 4 Apr, 2017, at 12:20 pm, Sir David Tang <dt@dwctang.com> wrote:

- I am not sure if I have another copy of the Cuban book! In fact I know I only have one copy myself. You should never never never lend out an important book! I never never never do!
- You will never find another copy. I have the original and I had 10 copies made and gave you one and others the rest. It was grim because every single

DT at opera street eatery / David 在粵劇節的路邊小吃攤

我屬牛，像隻牛在賣瓷器的商店裡，好幾年沒有來
Tokyo Hands，買了一堆很棒的東西要送給朋友！
HM

世界上我最喜歡的店！
Sir David Tang

27 Dec 2016, 22:09, How Man <hmwong@cers.org.hk> 寫：
親愛的爵士，
謝謝你的新書，我剛從《中國會》收到。

他在一本親筆簽名書裡寫著：「給 How Man，我們這世
代唯一一位真正的中國探險家—— David Tang」。多大
的讚美，尤其是從一位對外傲慢的人，但是對內，會選
擇性的謙虛，特別是對年長的人。

23 Dec, 2016, 5:10 am, Sir David Tang <dt@dwctang.com> 寫：
我都不知道要用你給我這 3 封 *email* 的哪一封！總之我剛
回到香港就看到你這些書，很期待閱讀它們。什麼時候可
以寄給你企鵝出版上個月幫我出版的書？
可以見個面嗎？我應該會待到 1 月 9 日。

Sir David Tang

Chinese complained. Every one!

- 18th but I leave again 21st! Back Feb 1,

I bought your book on Tibet the other day and gave it to Pippa Middleton,

sister-in-law of Prince William!

On 30 Dec 2016, at 12:05, How Man <hmwong@cers.org.hk> wrote from Japan:

As I am an Ox, I'm like a bull in a China shop now, not having been at Tokyo Hands for a few years, buying up all the neat stuff, for friends!

HM

My favouritest shop in the world!

Sir David Tang

On 27 Dec 2016, at 22:09, How Man <hmwong@cers.org.hk> wrote:

Dear Sir,

Thank you for your new book, which I just received from the China Club.

One of his signed books was scripted, "For How Man, The only real China explorer of our age, David Tang." What a compliment from someone who is outwardly arrogant, and inwardly, selectively humble, especially with modesty when reaching out to elderlies.

On 23 Dec, 2016, at 5:10 am, Sir David Tang <dt@dwctang.com> wrote:

November 17, 2016 David 寫：

我親愛的朋友，你好嗎？

我在英國接受醫療，恐怕 12 月中後才能回到香港。我的
好朋友羅素 · 克洛有位朋友艾利 · 愛肯會去香港，我
知道她會跟你見面。我希望你可以好好地招待她，羅素的
好朋友就是我的好朋友。如果你們兩位都有空的話，請你
帶她去《中國會》吃午餐或晚飯，我請客。我也會把這封
信給羅素。

Sir David Tang 口述

2015 年到 2017 年之間的通信：

－ 噯呀我會在醫院

－ 真的好戲劇化。唉，我在倫敦下周準備要做髖關節置
換手術。所以可能要到五月才能回到香港。但是我們一定
要盡快安排一起吃個午餐或晚飯。我的辦公室，我已經訂
了兩台最新的乒乓球機。

－ 真的好久不見。唉我被留在倫敦因為有另一個癌症手
術。我 11 月 4 日住院。真的不知道什麼時候會回來。

Sir David Tang

I never know which e mail I should use of the 3 I have of you! Anyway I have just come back to hongkong and found your brace of books which I look forward to reading. To where can I send you mine which was published by Penguin last month?

Might we see each other? I should be around until Jan 9.

Sir David Tang

On November 17, 2016 David wrote:

How are you, my dear friend?

I am afraid I have had some medical treatment in the UK, and won't be back in Hong Kong until mid-December. But my very good friend, Russell Crowe, has a friend called Ellie Aitken coming to visit Hong Kong, and I understand that she is coming to meet you. I hope you will look after her as any friend of Russell is a friend of mine. If both of you have time, please take her to the China Club for lunch or dinner with my compliments. I am copying this email to Russell.

Dictated by Sir David Tang

Several exchanges between 2015 and 2017:

- Alas I will be in hospital

- What drama indeed. Alas, I am in London from next week prepar-

我們最近的一次午餐約在《中國會》，還有我的朋友包括菲律賓總領事 Catella，David 看起來好像鬆了一口氣，他的《中國會》才剛跟中國銀行續了 6 年的租約。接下來就是 David Tang 非常典型的一陣罵，在這裡不宜刊出，主要是關於要提供專屬的樓層、電梯給大樓業主，還要有一間特殊的包廂給他們私人銀行家使用。

在 15 樓的《中國會》裡面有個收藏中國書籍的圖書館，非常的特別，也很出名，但是很少人使用。也只有少數幾位會員跟客人知道，在走道最後一排靠長廊的櫃子裡，那些音樂書籍是 Sir David Tang 的私人收藏，他對古典音樂的知識很深厚。音樂是他這一輩子的喜好，常常會出現在他的文字裡，並巧妙地出現在金融時報的專欄中。

這一點可以從今年 4 月 26 日我跟 David 的一封通信看得出來，我剛去義大利的克雷莫納。

你寫的這篇關於 Stradivarius 的文章非常棒！

5 月 4 日我很想加入我太太跟一位家裡的客人。我可以請你吃晚飯嗎？《中國會》應該比潮江春來得有氣氛？你只要告訴我幾個人。

ing for my hip replacement surgery. So might not be back in Hong-
kong until May. But definitely we should have lunch or dinner soonest!
My office, I think, have ordered both of the up-graded versions of the ping-
pong machine.
- Long time no see indeed. But alas I am going to be detained by another
cancer surgery in London. I go into hospital on Nov 4. And don't really know
when I will be back.

Sir David Tang

At one of our recent lunches at the China Club with my friends, including
Consul General Catella of the Philippines, David seemed relieved to have just
finalized a renewed lease for the China Club with a six years contract with the
Bank of China. It was followed by classic David Tang barrage of profanity,
not printable here, about having to designate a floor to floor elevator for the
building owner and a special room assigned for their private banker's priority
use.

The library of books on China on the 15th floor of the China Club is unique
and famous, though rarely used. But few members or guests realize that along
the last aisle against a walled corridor are shelves of books on music, part of
Sir David's private collection, which reflected his deep knowledge of classical

我 50 歲生日的時候去不丹，跟皇后去老虎的窩。約克公爵夫人還有她的兩位女兒也跟我一起，還有，當然約克公爵上的學校跟約克公爵是同一所！

Sir David Tang

收到我的正面回應後，他又寫：

非常謝謝你。我會帶我太太跟一位家裡的客人 *Aly Van den Berg*，是一位雕塑家，還有約克公爵夫人，安德魯王子的前妻，她到現在還跟他住在一起！她跟我一起去不丹，帶著她兩位公主女兒 *Beatrice* 和 *Eugenie*，我們跟皇后一起去老虎窩。我們總共會有 13 位。我們都是華人，所以對這個不迷信。

Sir David Tang 口述

那天晚餐我的客人是不丹的 *Kesang* 公主和錫金的 *Pema* 公主，所以一共是 16 個人，下面這張照片跟標題是 *David* 在 5 月 5 日寄給我的。

music. That life-long love of his often finds a place in his writings and crept into his FT column appropriately.

It is reflected in another exchange I had with David earlier this year on April 26 after my visit to Cremona in Italy.

I have read your excellent article on Stradivarius!

On May 4 I'd love to join with my wife and a house guest. Can I not host the dinner for you? The China Club might be a bit more atmospheric than Chiu Chow Gardens? You just have to let me know numbers.

I went up tigers nests with the Queen when I was in Bhutan for my 50th birthday. The Duchess of York and her two girls were there with me and of course the Duke of York went to the same school as the Duke of York!

Sir David Tang

Upon my answer to the positive, he further wrote:

Thank you very much. I am bringing my wife and our house guest Aly Van den

DT & HM co-host princesses and guests recently /
DT 與 HM 近期一起接待公主與賓客

Berg who is a sculptor – and the Duchess of York, ex-wife of Prince Andrew with whom she still lives! She came to Bhutan with me and walked up Tiger's Nest with her two daughters Princesses Beatrice and Eugenie – together with the Queen at the time. So there will be 13 of us. As we are Chinese, we are not superstitious!

Dictated by Sir David Tang

And that dinner for my guests Princess Kesang of Bhutan and Princess Pema of Sikkim turned out to be a party for 16, with a picture and captions that David sent to me below on May 5.

----**Original Message**-----

From: Sir David Tang [mailto:dt@dwctang.com]

Sent: Friday, 5 May 2017 2:39 PM

To: How Man <hmwong@cers.org.hk>

Subject:

I think a very jolly time was had by all! Thank you for bringing to us your lovely friends!

David, as I'm writing this on a flight from Los Angeles to Hong Kong, I intend

----Original Message-----

From: Sir David Tang [mailto:dt@dwctang.com]

Sent: Friday, 5 May 2017 2:39 PM

To: How Man <hmwong@cers.org.hk>

<u>我想大家都度過了一個非常愉快的時光！謝謝你帶來這麼可愛的朋友！</u>

David，我在從洛杉磯回香港的飛機上寫這篇文章，我想要寄一封到你的信箱，也許你正在看 Agony Uncle 專欄的讀者來信。唉，但是這個週六當我拿到週末版的金融時報時，我再也不會馬上翻到你專欄的那一版。

生命就像鋼琴
白色鍵代表快樂
黑色鍵代表哀傷
但是當你走在人生的道路上
記得黑色的鍵
也是會創造音樂的

DT on piano / David 彈鋼琴

to send it to your email just in case you are still reading letters to your Agony Uncle column. Alas, for this Saturday, I would no longer turn first to the section with your column when I lay my hands on the Weekend FT.

Life is like a piano
the white keys
represent happiness
and the black shows
sadness. but as you
go through life's
journey, remember
that the black keys
also makes music.

我的帝國大廈片刻

MY EMPIRE STATE
MOMENT

New York – September 13, 2017

我的帝國大廈片刻

我考慮拋下我的 *iPhone* 創造歷史，但是很快地，被拋下的是這個「想法」。畢竟這是兩年前一位朋友送我的生日禮物。

我小心翼翼地往前傾，從高得令人頭暈的 *103* 樓的陽台往下面的街道看，這裡的陽台並沒有防護柵欄。其實我的手機若是掉下去的話也不會落在第 *5* 大道，頂多只會到 *86* 樓的陽台。帝國大廈每年有超過 *4* 百萬遊客來到這裡觀賞曼哈頓還有大紐約市的 *360* 度景觀。

帝國大廈幾乎佔據了第 *5* 大道和 *34* 街整個街區。這座摩天大廈的圓形觀景台周長大約只有 *55* 呎。「摩天大廈」我突然重新思考這個我閱讀、也使用了幾十年的字，思考它真正的意思。這一刻正可以定義這個字。

還有哪裡可以讓人在 *55* 步之內，可以將整個紐約市盡收眼底。稱它全景似乎太過輕描淡寫。應該要有

MY EMPIRE STATE MOMENT

I considered dropping my iPhone and making history, but quickly dropped, instead, the thought. After all, it was a birthday gift from a friend two years ago.

I gingerly leaned forward to look, from the dizzying height of the 103rd floor balcony with no protective fence, at the streets below. My phone would not have hit the street on 5th Avenue. At best, only on the balcony of the 86th floor of the Empire State Building, where each year over four million visitors take in the breathtaking panorama of Manhattan and of greater New York City beyond.

The footprint of the Empire State Building is almost a full block around from 5th Avenue and 34th Street. Up on top of the towering skyscraper and just below the antenna, the circular balcony was maybe only fifty feet in circumference. "Skyscraper" … I suddenly reconsider the real meaning of this word that I have read and used for decades. This is a defining moment of the word.

新創的字來形容這種感覺。聖母峰大廈 (The Everest of Building)？畢竟字裡有「-est」代表最高級的。這並不是關於高度，是感覺。身為一位探險家，我在西藏上到過令人頭昏的高度。但是這個真的不一樣。

這是新認識的朋友 Tony Malkin 招待的，他是帝國房地產信託公司的主席。他的兒子 George 去年來香港，剛好遇到他的生日，我幫他過生日。算不上是個生日派對，只有畢尉林博士、我，還有 George，三個人在我們海邊的石澳展覽館裡的廚房，George 對著一塊小蛋糕上

Entrance icon on Ground Floor / 一樓的圖像

Where else can one take less than fifty careful steps, breath-holding steps, and at the same time take in the full breadth of New York City. Calling it a panorama is an understatement. Some new vocabulary is needed to describe the feeling. The Everest of Buildings? Maybe. After all, "-est" makes a superlative. It's not the height, but the feeling. As an explorer, I've been on other dizzying heights in Tibet. And this is different, "dif-fe-rent".

This is a special treat from a new friend Tony Malkin, Chairman of the Empire State Realty Trust. I thank myself for having hosted his son George when he passed through Hong Kong a year ago on his birthday. Not much of a party,

Art Deco Ground level / 一樓的藝術裝飾

Floor 103 / 103 樓

的蠟燭吹。很簡單,就跟我現在在帝國大廈的頂樓一
樣。

兩位接待 VIP 的導遊跟著我。他們身穿酒紅色的制服讓
這次的拜訪變得有點正式。Patricia 和 Hugo 帶我穿過滿
滿都是遊客的一樓,然後進到一部沒有人的電梯裡。換
過兩部電梯後,我們在 86 樓進到一台老式電梯,像手
風琴一樣可以收縮的門跟一個手把可以開關門。很快地

just George, Dr. Bleisch and myself, as George quietly blew out the single candle on a small cake in the kitchen of our house in Shek O by the beach. Just as simple as now on top of the Empire State Building.

Two escorts for VIPs were with me. Their burgundy uniforms made the visit a bit more formal. Patricia and Hugo led me past all the lines of tourists on the ground floor and ushered me into a special elevator with no one else. Two changes of elevators later, we entered an old manually operated elevator on the 86th floor, with accordion-like iron draw gate and a handle to open and close the door. We quickly arrived at the 102nd floor where there was an enclosed balcony. We did not even stop where tourists pay extra to have a privileged and secured view from the glass-enclosed deck.

Patricia was holding two keys on an elastic chain. She opened a secure small door revealing a steep metal staircase against the door. We climbed up holding the handrails. "Please be careful," Hugo repeated twice. Twenty feet higher and we ascended to this tiny room filled with exposed brass piping and electric boxes. This is the access room to the radio antenna above the building. Many radio stations broadcasted from the 86th to 101st floors, and their antennas are all on top of the Empire State.

Here was located a heavy metal door with glass, similar to those on ancient boats. There were two padlocks plus a handle lock on top. "It must be heavily

我們來到 102 樓，這裡的陽台是封閉的。這個樓層是必須要加付費才可以上來的，遊客可以透過玻璃帷幕盡覽高樓風光。

Patricia 手上的塑膠鑰匙鍊上掛著兩把鑰匙。她打開一扇門，門後是金屬階梯。我們握住欄杆往上走。「請小心！」Hugo 說了兩次。爬了 20 呎高我們來到一個小房間，裡面堆滿了氧化的銅管還有電箱。這裡可以通往這棟建築上的電台天線。有許多電台從 86 樓到 101 樓放送廣播，他們的天線都在帝國大廈的頂樓。

眼前出現一道厚重金屬門，門上還有片玻璃，很像古代船上的門，金屬門上還加了兩個掛鎖。「這道門一定要鎖得很緊，因為上頭的風很大。」Patricia 說。我們越過

George birthday c. G. Malkin / George Malkin 的生日

secured, because the wind can be brutal up here," said Patricia. We stepped through the door, a door that unlocked a view unmatched anywhere in the Big Apple.

"Huh? Is that the Chrysler Building?" I asked looking down at that famous Art Deco icon. "Yes, indeed it is," answered Hugo. I knew this was a very privileged visit given the old and rustic look of the door and locks, compared to the posh and shiny décor of the entire trip up to this point. "How many times have you been up here?" I turned to Patricia and asked. "Twice in my seven years as special guide to VIPs," came her answer.

"How about you?" I turned to Hugo and asked. "Three times in my eleven years," came the answer. So five times in 18 years added together! No wonder even my guides seemed thrilled in escorting me. I have always pitied tour guides in how frequently they have to repeat walking tours through exhibits, but obviously these two guides didn't mind a damn bit about walking through this exhibit. This was Exhibit Z, the last and only one.

I've often said, "If you want to be Number One, you need size. But if you want to be the Only One, you go small." It manifested itself right there, going from Number One to Only One, a metaphor of that single tall candle on a birthday cake, as I ascended The Empire State to its top. To describe what it feels like to be the Only One would be frivolous. It is a feeling to oneself!

了這道門，門後揭開的景觀是這顆大蘋果裡獨一無二的。

「咦？那是克萊斯勒大樓嗎？」我看著下面這棟有名的藝術裝置地標問。「是的，那棟就是！」Hugo 回答。我很清楚能上到這裡來的機會是萬分難得的，那道老舊生鏽的門跟鎖，跟一路上來都是光鮮亮麗的裝飾這兩者有很大的差異。「你上來過這裡幾次？」我轉過去問 Patricia。「我這 7 年來在這裡擔任 VIP 的指定導遊，但也只上來過兩次！」她這樣回答。

「那你呢？」我轉過去問 Hugo。「11 年來共 3 次。」這是他的答案。所以加起來 18 年一共 5 次！難怪連帶我的導遊都好興奮。我一直都覺得導遊很可憐，必須不停的重複導覽內容，但是顯然的這兩位導遊一點也不介意帶我看這景觀。這個是展覽 Z，最後的一個，也是唯一的一個。

我常說，「如果你想要當第一名，那要比大小。但是如果你要成為唯一的，那你就專注在小的」。我一邊爬上帝國大廈的最頂端一邊想著，這兒就是最好的例子，從第一名到唯一的，就好像那支插在生日蛋糕上面的蠟燭。如果試圖形容唯一的那種感覺恐怕會顯得輕浮。但，這感受確實是非常個人的！

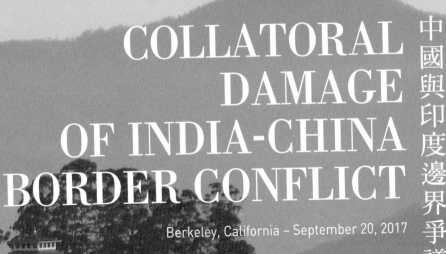

COLLATORAL DAMAGE OF INDIA-CHINA BORDER CONFLICT

中國與印度邊界爭議的連帶傷害

Berkeley, California – September 20, 2017

中國與印度邊界爭議的連帶傷害

「有人敲門，」Yin-chin 回顧那天在她大吉嶺家發生的事。「然後三個穿卡其色制服的男人進來命令我們立刻要搬走。他們只給我們短短的一個鐘頭打包行李。」

「我才剛滿 13 歲而母親在加德滿都創業，父親幾個禮拜前被帶到當地的監獄服刑。我做了最壞的打算，一邊翻父親的抽屜，拿走三支歐米茄跟一支勞力士手錶，心想我們一人可以戴一支，然後一邊打包行李。這些手錶是父親做進出口生意的東西。我弟弟 Bobby 才 8 歲，外婆 Popo 纏了小腳，他們手上都會戴一支手錶。我心想可能會用得上。」Yin 坐在我的對面，我們在她的柏克萊山丘的家，望出去可以看到舊金山海灣。

「我才剛開始有月經，所以匆忙地將衛生棉也打包。」Yin 又說。不過那些衛生棉都沒有派上用場，因為之後的創傷打亂了她的經期，長達 5 個月。

COLLATORAL DAMAGE
OF INDIA-CHINA BORDER CONFLICT

"There was a knock on the door," Yin-Chin recounted what happened one day at her home in Darjeeling. *"Three men in khaki uniform entered and ordered that we would be moved away at once. We were instructed that we had one hour to pack our belongings."*

"I had just turned thirteen and my mother had been away to Kathmandu to start a new business, and my father had been taken away to a local prison a few weeks before. I feared for the worst and shuffled through my father's drawers, chose three Omegas and a Rolex watch for each of us to wear while packing my bags. These were items from his import-export business.   My

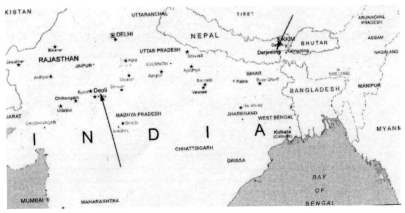

Map of Darjeeling to Rajasthan / 大吉嶺到拉賈斯坦的地圖

Darjeeling prison / 大吉嶺監獄

Yin 從此開始一段少為人知的旅程，她從喜馬拉雅山下被遷到千里之外拉賈斯坦邦的沙漠，被安置在 Deoli 城外的一座監獄裡，那是一座收容了 2 千多名中國人的監獄。經過一番苦難，Yin 與父親重逢了，他們四個人被放在同一間平房，叫「平房二號」，在英國殖民時代曾經關過尼赫魯。諷刺的是，這次的刑期是由尼赫魯下令的，當時他是印度獨立後第一任總理！

那年是 1962 的 12 月，中國與印度邊界的戰爭開打。事實上，有兩千多名的中國人生活居住在印度北邊的大吉嶺到阿薩姆這個區域，有些人甚至出生在這裡。雖然中國跟印度邊界的衝突只有一個月左右，但影響所及讓有些中國人竟然被拘禁長達五年。曾經在這個區域生活的

brother Bobby, who was eight, and grandmother Popo, with bound feet, would each wear one watch. I thought it may come in handy," Yin said sitting across from me at her home in the Berkeley hills overlooking San Francisco Bay.

"I had just started my period. So I made haste to pack also my sanitary napkins," Yin added. But it turned out to be not of much use, as the traumatic experience that followed disrupted her period for the next five months.

Thus began an odyssey seldom told and little known to the outside world, as Yin was moved a thousand miles away from the foothills of the Himalayas into the desert of Rajasthan, to a prison camp outside of the town of Deoli, among over two thousand Chinese internees. By fortitude, Yin rejoined her father, and the four of them were put in the same bungalow, "Bungalow 2", once used for confinement of Nehru, during the time of British rule. Ironically, this time the prison term was imposed by Nehru himself, now founding president of India.

The year was December 1962. A border war had just started between India and China. Over 2,500 Chinese who lived, and made their living in northern India from Darjeeling to Assam, some having been born there, would end up interned in that camp; some for up to five years, long after the one-month border conflict had settled down. Today many of these Chinese have successfully immigrated overseas, repatriated to China, or moved to Taiwan. But some would remain stateless, never allowed to return to their former

中國人很多後來都移民到國外，然後再回到中國，或是移民台灣。但是也有一些人長期處於無國籍的狀態，他們失去財產，也沒有辦法回到老家。直到現在他們每年都要去跟官方報到，付費，以取得暫時的居留許可。

Yin 和她的弟弟是幸運的少數。他們的母親不久後跟先生離婚，然後跟一位美國外交官交往。透過一位外國記者的調解，那位記者曾威脅要揭露那所關押邊境中國人的監獄，這招終於讓尼赫魯居服。被關了兩個月之後，這對兩姊弟終於被釋放。不過這段日子的折磨影響了 *Yin* 一輩子，直到不久前她才願意把這段不為人知的傷痛書寫出來。

這可以被視為是中印邊界衝突所產生的連帶傷害。戰爭只維持了一個月，卻破壞了兩國關係長達半世紀之久，而在 *Yin* 心裡所烙下的，更是一輩子的傷痕。

國防部長和將軍們在各自的首都或是現場指揮所，他們坐在舒適的辦公室、戰爭室裡發號司令，像賭場裡的賭徒，輸的是鈔票而不是他們的生命。他們的決定或許是基於戰略推理，可以是真實，也可能只是想像。也或許是一種民族主義，是現狀或是歷史的。更說不定只是為了轉移新聞焦點，甚至可能是推估自己或敵

homes. All their fortunes and properties were lost, and to this day they must still report to authorities each year, to pay to acquire some interim registration papers.

Yin and her brother were two of the fortunate ones. Their mother, who would soon divorce their father, started dating an American diplomat, and through the mediation of a foreign reporter, who threatened to expose the internment of the Chinese, successfully wrestled Nehru into letting go of the two children after two months in prison. But the ordeal had a life-long impact on Yin, and only recently would she write about her traumatic experience and let her past be known.

Such may be considered collateral damage of the India-China border conflict. While the war lasted only a month, the disruption of the two countries' relationship lasted more than half a century, and scarred Yin for a lifetime.

Defense ministers and generals sitting in comfortable position in their government offices and war rooms in respective capitals or field command posts make a call to battle, not unlike gamblers at casino tables losing paper money, but not their lives. Their decision could be based on strategic reasons, real or imagined, or nationalism, current or historic, or perhaps a diversion of national interests from other news at a specific moment, or even just a spur of the moment anxiety in second-guessing their own strength or those of their

人實力時，因為焦慮所產生的一時衝動。這種事很難被外人理解和分析。

對於中國的前線歷史、政治和動態，長久以來我從遠處，也就近觀察，甚至親自前往中印邊境。30 多年來，我走訪喜馬拉雅山的兩側，還有沿著邊境的國家。

我曾從令人發暈的高海拔接觸喜馬拉雅山和喀喇崑崙山好多次，我的足跡從阿克賽欽地區，到中國控制的邊境 K2 區再到中印共同擁有的班公湖。我也曾到過邊境那

Road crossing Aksa Chin / 穿越阿克賽欽的道路

enemy's. Such matters are difficult for any outsiders to fathom, explain and analyze.

As a long-time student of China's frontiers history, politics and dynamics, I have long observed from a distance in time, as well as close-up in physical presence, the India-China border. I have, over the last thirty years or so, visited both sides of the Himalayas and its bordering countries.

From the dizzying heights of the western Himalayas and the Karakoram, I have seen, on several occasions, the Aksai Chin, from the Chinese controlled

Graves of Chinese & Ughur soldiers / 中國與維族士兵的墓

裡做訪 1962 年戰爭喪命的中國解放軍墓地。

我去過措那，靠近最具爭議並由印度控制的達旺。我也進到錫金與不丹邊境的亞東和帕里，以及珞巴族所在的米林縣，它位於邊境的中間。我也一路直達察隅，那是爭議邊境的最東角落。在印度這一邊，我的行動受到比較多的限制，不過我還是去了拉達克和錫金，曾經是個王國如今成為印度的一部分。

自從印度在 1959 年收容達賴喇嘛和他的流亡政府後，這件事對中印關係產生巨大的影響。情況惡化到在邊境開戰直到 1962 年底結束。雖然戰爭只維持了一個月，在冬季來到喜馬拉雅高山前結束，但是後果卻是久遠的。好幾位作家、學者和軍事專家都曾寫過關於這場雖然短暫但卻影響深遠的戰爭。有些甚至寫到印度錯失有利的機會去解決邊境爭議，如果他們曾經注意到中國在 1950 年代處理與緬甸和尼泊爾的問題時的大方態度。

當時西方世界正處於反共產主義，中國被視為侵略者。印度才剛獨立 15 年，還處在建立國家的認同和主權的完整上，卻承襲了已經離去的大英帝國思想。他們更是低估了中國解放軍，這一支經歷過二戰，長期的內戰，甚至在韓戰中與美國勢均力敵的軍隊。1962 年的戰役

frontier of K2 region to the jointly held lake, Bangong Co. I have even paced the cemetery holding remains of PLA soldiers immortalized by the 1962 war along this border.

I have visited Cona, near the contested border with Tawang on the Indian-controlled side, Yadong and Phari by the Sikkim - Bhutan border, the Lhoba-inhabited region in Miling at the mid-section of the frontier, all the way to Zayu on the eastern section of the frontier in contention. On the Indian side, my mobility has been more restricted. Nonetheless, I have visited Ladakh and also Sikkim, a former kingdom turned Indian state.

India's has harbored the Dalai Lama and his exiled government since 1959, which must have been a most detrimental turning point in the China-India relationship. It deteriorated into open war on several fronts toward the end of 1962. Though the battles lasted only a month before winter set in in the high Himalayas, the implication has been long lasting. Several writers, both scholarly and military, have written about that short but momentous war. Some even mentioned the missed opportunity on the Indian side to settle the border issue to their advantage, had they taken notice of China's generous settlement of its border with Burma (Myanmar) and Nepal during the 1950s.

At the time, under the Red scare in the western world, China was looked upon as the aggressor. India, barely 15 years into independence, was trying

讓印軍蒙羞，陰影一直持續至今。

後來成為學者的記者 Neville Maxwell，在取得印度方面的內部機密文件後，一改之前他對於 1962 年這場戰爭的看法，證實印方的推進政策導致中國沒有談判的空間。訊息揭露的 8 年後，也就是 1970 年，中國終於被證實不是侵略者或始作俑者。事實上，那場戰役發生的時間中國正處於最艱困的時候，它根本沒有餘力去發動戰爭，因為那時的時空背景正是大躍進，經濟與農業都出現很大的問題。

to establish its own national identity and integrity, taking on some of the residual empire mentality of the departing British. It further underestimated a war-hardened People's Liberation Army after WWII, a prolonged civil war, and even a draw with the US and international forces at the Korean War. The 1962 conflict ended with the humiliation of the Indian Army which has a long shadow to the present day.

One reporter turned scholar, Neville Maxwell, stood up and changed his stand on the 1962 border conflict after acquiring some secret and confidential internal documents from the Indian side, testifying to India's advance policy which left no room for negotiation with China. His expose eight years later in 1970 thus redeemed a lot of merit for China as not being the initial aggressor/instigator. In fact, the war happened during China's hardest time, when she could ill-afford to wage a war, during the financial and agricultural set-backs of the Great Leap Forward.

Fast forward a couple years. Maxwell's book had the unintended value of allowing Kissinger, and later President Nixon, to pursue a more open policy with China. After reading Maxwell's account, Kissinger is quoted as saying, "If that's how the Chinese are, we can deal with them."

For the next fifty or so years, the old wound of the India-China War dictated much of India's foreign policy among its many Himalayan neighbors. It

Ladakh / 拉達克

快轉兩年。不是作者的原意，但是 Maxwell 的書卻讓季辛吉和後來的尼克森對中國的政策比較開放。在閱讀過 Maxwell 的書之後，季辛吉曾說：「如果中國人是這樣的話，那我們可以跟他們來往。」

接下來的 50 多年，中印戰爭的舊傷口影響印度與喜馬拉雅山邊境國的外交政策。它接著更鞏固印度對錫金和不丹的強勢政策。中國對西藏的強硬手段和文化大革命，更加深了鄰國向印度的靠攏。除了巴基斯坦之外，因為他們與印度也有領土的問題。

喜馬拉雅山的地質結構，是三千年來兩個大陸板塊的地震撞擊的產物。最近這裡的爭議又升到沸點，就在中國和不丹的邊界。不丹世襲的君主，旺楚克家族之子，被封為不丹的第一位君主，而第一位國王被英國封為尤恩‧旺楚克爵士。他和英屬印度的關係很好，親自參與支持 1904 年英國軍隊進入拉薩，也在後來的和平協議中扮演重要的角色。

近幾十年來，不丹很難拿捏該怎麼對外開放以取得國際認同，但又不讓印度提高緊覺，畢竟它是受印度保護的。錫金在 1974 年的結局給了不丹一個無言的教訓，也是不丹想要避免的。中國和不丹有個很特別的關係。

certainly further consolidated its hold on Sikkim and hardened its policy on Bhutan. China's strong-hand approach in Tibet and the devastating Cultural Revolution also further pushed countries on its periphery into the orbit of India, with the exception, of course of, Pakistan which had its own score to settle with India.

Recently, the tectonics of the Himalayas, that product of the 30-million-year-old seismic crashing of two continents, is again rising to a boiling point, this time simmering in a piece of land bordering the kingdom of Bhutan and China. The hereditary monarch of Bhutan, a son of the Wangchuk family, was endorsed as the first Maharaja of Bhutan when its first king was knighted by the British as Sir Ugyen Wangchuk. His well established relationship with British India put him in good stead, as he personally met and supported the British forced march to Lhasa in 1904, as well as playing a role in the subsequent peace treaty.

In more recent decades, Bhutan has had a difficult balancing act to play as it attempted to open as much international recognition and space for the kingdom as possible without raising alarm from India, being its protector state. The 1974 fortitude and the end of the kingdom of Sikkim set an unsaid example for Bhutan to try and avoid. China has a very different relationship with Bhutan. While there are more than a dozen roads from India into Bhutan, not one single road is open from its huge neighbor to the

從印度到不丹的路徑超過一打，但卻沒有一條是通往北方的鄰國的。歷史上進不丹的路可是要經過西藏綽莫拉日神山旁的帕里。中國這個曾經是政治上可怕的巨人，在二十年間變成不可忽視的巨大經濟體。

中國與不丹的邊境之爭已經談判了不下 20 回，是以友善及文明的方式，在印度的眼皮底下進行的。穩定與堅定的不丹，與中國有良好的關係，不會被視為對印度有

north, though the historical road to enter Bhutan was through Phari in Tibet next to the sacred Mount Cholmolari. Still, China, which was once a much-feared political behemoth, has turned in the last two decades into a financial powerhouse that cannot be ignored.

Rapprochement to settle some points of border dispute between Bhutan and China had gone on for almost twenty rounds in amicable and cordial ways, under the watchful eyes and cautious behind-the-scene influence of India. A stable and assertive Bhutan, especially one with a friendly relationship with China, would not be looked upon as benefiting India's national interest. An invisible hand can at times be seen in many aspects of Bhutan's foreign policy, as well as its internal politics. The long litany of historic intrigues between the Wangchuk and Dorji families are well known to historians and scholars of Bhutan.

The recent publication of a memoir, titled "A Life in Diplomacy", by India's former Foreign Secretary Maharajakhrisna Rasgotra is a case in point. It seems hardly diplomatic, as in his claim that Lhendup Dorji, then acting as Prime Minister of Bhutan after his brother's assassination as former Prime Minister, sent his emissary to ask for support in an attempted coup to overthrow the Wangchuk dynasty during the reign of the Third King of Bhutan. Lhendup, long dead, cannot rise to refute the accusation.

益。事實上，有一隻隱形的手在操控不丹的外交政策和國內政治。不丹的歷史學家和學者都很清楚旺楚克和道爾吉家族在歷史上的關係。

最近出版的一個回憶錄《A Life in Diplomacy》就是很好的例子，這本由印度前任的外交部長 Maharajakhrisna Rasgotra 撰寫。他聲稱當時不丹的總理 Lhendup Dorji，曾派出使者尋求發動政變，以推翻不丹第三位國王的旺楚克王朝。Lhendrup 早已不在人世，沒辦法站出來否認這項指控。事實上，Lhendup Dorji 的哥哥是前任的總理，是被暗殺後才由弟弟接任的。

這讓 Dorji 皇太后的母親，也是錫金的公主非常的生氣，發了聲明譴責這毫無根據的指控。Ashi Kesang Choden Wangchuk 皇太后是第四位國王的母親，兒子於 2008 年退位交棒給他的兒子，現在的第五位國王。這位印度外交部長所披露的不管是真的還是假想的，確實已經讓向來平靜的國度造成不必要的內部猜疑了。

最近的僵局似乎也有道理，起因是中國在 Doklam 也稱 Dongland 靠不丹的邊境修造馬路，這讓印度跟中國爭論不休，兩個大國互相指控大開口水戰。中印雙方軍隊對峙長達兩個月，對峙的地點居然不是在中國與印度之

Thus it was left to a very upset Royal Grandmother, a Dorji and also a Princess of Sikkim, to write and denounce that "baseless" accusation. Ashi Kesang Choden Wangchuk, the Royal Grandmother, is mother to the Fourth King, who abdicated in 2008 to put his son in charge, now the Fifth King of Bhutan. The revelation by India's Foreign Minister, real or imagined, is certain to destabilize and upset a largely peaceful kingdom, creating unnecessary internal suspicion.

So it seems logical that in the recent impasse about Chinese roadbuilding at a site called Doklam or Donglang near the Bhutanese border became a dispute between India and China, with spats of accusation and mudslinging between the two giants. This though, the two-month face-off of soldiers of the two countries, happened on disputed Bhutan-China territory rather than along the now India-China, formerly Sikkim-China, frontier of Yadong.

Bhutan has effectively become a pawn, its own national and foreign policy hi-jacked by a powerful neighbor, only belatedly voicing its own displeasure by joining its "Big Brother" to the south. It is highly possible that the recent tension at the border is not targeting China, but an excuse for India to exert and demonstrate itself as proxy for the kingdom of Bhutan. The message is for the world to take notice, but especially for Bhutan. As I have noted before, big countries can afford to lose a war, but small countries cannot afford to win one. It would take forever to recover, if at all.

間，而是在不丹與中國的爭議領土，昔日的錫金─中國，亞東的前線。

不丹顯然是個棋子，國內和外交政策都被強大的鄰居劫持，遲遲到最近才說出他們的不滿而加入南方的「大哥哥」。很有可能最近邊境緊張的情勢不是針對中國，而是印度藉機來展現他們是不丹的代理人。這訊息值得全世界注意，尤其是不丹。我以前說過，大國輸得起戰爭，小國連打勝戰爭都承受不起。它們會需要非常久的時間復原，幾乎是不可能完全復原。

像 *Yin-Chin*，在 1962 年中印戰爭中成為連帶的傷害，不丹夾在兩個交戰的強大鄰居中間，也可能成為連帶的受害者。希望未來，中國與印度的領導人同時都有智慧，可以畫出共同的遠程目標，彼此和平相處。

他們必需要了解這些國家並沒有辦法搬走，不像 *Yin-Chin* 以及那些跟她一樣生出在印度，生活在印度的中國人。否則中國和印度自己在國際政治角力下都有可能會成為連帶受害者。

Like Yin-Chin, who became collateral damage of the India-China War of 1962, Bhutan is caught in the crossfire between two huge neighbors, very much a compromise, if not a sacrifice, as yet another bit of collateral damage. Hopefully in time, India and China will have leaders of wisdom simultaneously, such that they can help define their two countries joint long-term goals, and learn to live with each other in peace.

They must realize that neither country can move away geographically, unlike Yin-Chin and her fellow Chinese, who were born and lived in India. Otherwise both China and India may also become collateral damage, in a larger sphere of global contention of international power politics.

MINOR AGONY IN FOUNDING CERS

創立CERS的小小煩惱

Pasadena, California – September 19, 2017

創立 CERS 的小小煩惱

表彰 Caltech，它曾經也是我的垃圾桶

「6 號宮保雞丁，18 號照燒牛肉還有 24 號彩虹蝦。」電話另一端傳來一位男生的聲音。「等等，等等，你是打給誰？」我盡量很禮貌地詢問。「喔！這裡不是中國快餐嗎？」然後電話斷了。

「我要一個糖醋雞，一個四川蝦，不要太辣喔！」電話另一頭傳來女生甜美的聲音。「您打錯電話了，這裡不是餐廳噢。」我試著去掉口吻裡的酸味讓自己聽起來甜美。「喔很抱歉！」她道歉後掛了電話。

接到這些電話的時空背景是 1986 年，我的山間小屋位於洛杉磯國家森林內的米拉德峽谷，離加州的帕薩迪納很近。那時我剛離開美國國家地理雜誌，在友人的協助下，就在這個木屋裡，成立了非營利的組織：中國探險學會 (CERS)。接下來的幾年常有這樣的電話打來，直到 1994 年我搬回香港。

MINOR AGONY IN FOUNDING CERS

And the trashing, and then honoring, of Caltech

"Number six Kung Pao chicken, number eighteen teriyaki beef and number twenty four rainbow shrimp," said the male voice on the other end of the phone line. *"But, but, who are you calling?"* I tried to be polite. *"Oh sorry, isn't this China Express?"* came the voice. Then the line went dead.

"I'll take a sweet and sour chicken, and a hot Szechwan shrimp, oh please don't make it too hot," came a sweet, female voice over the phone. *"Ma'am, but you must have the wrong number, this is not a restaurant,"* I tried talking sweet and cut the sour. *"Oh I'm sorry!"* she apologized and hung up.

It was 1986 when I first began taking those calls from my mountain cabin at Millard Canyon inside Angeles National Forest, a short distance above and beyond Pasadena in California. I had just left the National Geographic Society and, with the help of a few friends, started the China Exploration & Research Society (CERS), a non-profit based in my cabin. For the next few years, until I moved to Hong Kong in 1994, such calls came in regularly.

成立 CERS 後幾個月我終於知道為什麼常常會接到這些電話。CERS 的電話號碼列在當地的電話簿裡，而接在我們後面的是一家叫 *China Express* 的快餐店，離山下的 *Lake Street* 約 10 分鐘的車程。很快地我也學會點我要

Soon after the first few months of incorporating CERS, I finally figured out why I was regularly receiving such calls. Listed in the local telephone book right under our number was China Express, a fast food restaurant ten minutes down the mountain on Lake Street. Before long, I learned to order

Millard trails / 米拉德步道

的 6 號餐，18 號和 24 號餐。每當我出發去中國，一趟就去了好幾個月，這些打來要訂餐的電話恐怕單子都沒人接吧。

這天一通電話打來，對方很大聲也很不客氣甚至口氣帶些威脅：「你是住在 Chaney Trail 的黃先生？你不要再把垃圾放到我的垃圾桶了！」男子大聲吼。「我在垃圾堆裡翻了翻才找到你的號碼！」他繼續說。我的郵件信封上透露了我的身分。

國家森林裡總共只有 14 個木屋。鄰居多是假日過來露

Millard Canyon neighbors / 米拉德峽谷的鄰居

my own Number 6, 18 and 24, so on and so forth. Perhaps during those years whenever I left for China for months at a time, many orders by phone to my number were unfilled, or unfulfilled!

One day, another surprising call came through, this time quite loud, hostile, and somewhat threatening. "Are you Mr. Wong living on Chaney Trail? You better stop putting your trash in my dumpster!" yelled the man. "I had to dig through your trash to get to you," he continued. The postal envelopes among my trash gave him my identity.

There were only 14 cabins inside the National Forest. Our neighbors were weekend campers and a volunteer family living in the Campground as caretaker. We cabin owners all lived in our houses on government leased land, with leases up to ten years, renewed practically automatically. We were a bunch of different, and at times strange, people. Most of us used the cabins for weekends. I was one exception who used it year round, except when I was overseas in China, while setting it up as the first home for CERS.

Among us were top-notch scientists from Caltech and NASA's Jet Propulsion Lab. Richard Feynman, perhaps the best known Nobel Physicist, was among the cabin owners. One other, Don Conlan, a friend now for 30 years, was President of Capital Group, a financial institution in a class by itself.

營的，還有一戶人家住在營地，是這裡的志工負責管理這營區。木屋主人都是住在自己的房子裡，但是地是跟政府承租的，租約可達 10 年，到期後幾乎都是自動續約。在那個時候我們是一群不太一樣的人，甚至有些奇怪。大多數的屋主只有在週末過來，只有我幾乎整年都在這個 CERS 的第一個家，除了去中國的時候。

住在這裡很多位是來自 Caltech 和 NASA 噴氣推進實驗室的頂尖科學家。其中最出名的一位是諾貝爾物理學家 Richard Feynman。另外一位是 Don Conlan，我認識他已經 30 年了，他曾經是 Capital Group 的主席，這個金融機構不僅歷史悠久，規模也是最大的。

原始自然的景觀環境是這裡最大的優點，但隨之而來的，是許多的不方便。木屋主人被要求要自己處理自己的垃圾，因為國家森林裡並沒有提供為住戶們收垃圾的服務。大多數的人還有除了這裡的住家，因此可以把垃圾帶回去那裡丟。但，這是我唯一的家，所以我會將垃圾包好丟到山下 Lake Street 一家便利商店的垃圾桶。顯然這家店的老闆並不覺得我這樣的行為對他很便利，所以氣到打電話給我。

Lake Street 下去幾英里就是加州理工學院 (Caltech)。這

Notwithstanding the advantages of having a pristine landscape and setting, there were inconveniences. Cabin owners were expected to take their trash out of their cabins and dump it themselves, as there was no trash service inside the National Forest for private residents. Most had a second, or actually a first, home to which to send their trash. I had none, thus found it most convenient to put my bagged trash at a dumpster behind a convenience store down the mountain, also on Lake Street. Apparently the owner of the store didn't find it that convenient, and thus the angry call to me.

A couple more miles down Lake was the California Institute of Technology, known as Caltech. That pantheon of science and technology was so exclusive that it only admitted about two hundred freshman students each year, making an undergrad population of about 800 students total. The graduate program was somewhat larger. Always among the top universities in the US despite its small size, Caltech claimed 34 Nobel Laureates, a ratio which would humble many much larger universities that often highlight their medalist count.

Since the late 1970s, I had often gone to Caltech to visit friends and professors. Some of my earliest exposure to satellite images came from Dr. Clarence Allen, the top seismologist at the time. Sam Lee, one of my best friends and a geochemist, traveled twice to China with me. Sam, like Dr. Allen, was also in the Geology building at Caltech.

所學校的科學和科技學院每年只收 200 名新生，學校總共大約有 800 名大學生。研究所的科系算是多一點的。加州理工學院是美國頂尖的學校，雖然它的規模很小，但是 Caltech 已經出了 34 位諾貝爾獎得主，這樣的紀錄讓許多喜歡彰顯獎章的大學校汗顏。

從 1970 年後期開始我常常去 Caltech 拜訪朋友和教授。我最早期接觸衛星影像是透過 Dr. Clarence Allen，他當時是位頂尖的地震學家。Sam Lee 是我最好的朋友之一，是位地球化學家，曾經兩次跟我去中國。他和 Dr. Allen 都在 Caltech 的同一棟地質學大樓。

從 1970 年初 Dr. Allen 就跟我分享陸地衛星多波段掃描影像，70 年代後期更與我分享 TM data。他對大地構造學非常有興趣，包括中國的地質，他在二戰之後第一次開始研究。他曾經飛越過青海的阿尼瑪卿山去那裡研究斷層。1980 年代中國開始開放之後，他也曾經前往四川的地震帶。每當這個地球有大地震發生的時候，他的辦公室外面就會聚集許多為了採訪他的電視台轉播車。就在他辦公室對面，有兩棟屬於美國地質調查局，專門負責監測全球地震活動的建築。

透過這樣的關係我對這附近的停車場變得很熟悉，還有

Caltech Geology building / Caltech 地質學大樓

It was Dr. Allen who shared with me Landsat MSS images from the early 1970s, and later TM data from the late 1970s and on. He had a huge interest in tectonics, including those in China, which he first studied after the Second World War. Dr. Allen revealed to me that he had flown over Amne Machin Mountain in Qinghai during the late 1940s to study fault lines. When China opened up in the 1980s, he visited a major earthquake region in western Sichuan. Whenever there was a major earthquake in the world, there would be several TV broadcasting trucks from different channels parked outside his office, beaming interviews with him. Across the street are two houses belonging to the US Geological Survey (USGS) which also monitors seismic movements around the world.

這裡的垃圾桶。很自然地這些垃圾桶變成我第二好的朋友，最好的朋友在大樓裡。稱這裡為「加州理工學院廢物丟棄點」好像有點不妥。不過在那個時候的確對我有很大的幫助。

Caltech 可是不能被當成廢物一樣丟棄，它可是提供剛在萌芽的 CERS 許多服務。1986 年學會成立後我們也曾接到除了叫外賣的其他電話，像是學生打來的，通常是研究生，還有一位教授 Dr. James Lee（李中清）。

James 的父親是李政道，在 1957 年和另一位中國物理學家一起獲得諾貝爾物理學獎。James 學的是中國歷史，後來卻在 Caltech 的學院任教。上他課的學生如果對中國少數民族地區有興趣的話，有時候會送到我那裡，因為這科是我的專長。

還有由 R. Stanton Avery 創辦的 Durfee 基金會，他在發明自黏貼標後創立了艾利丹尼森公司。1930 年代，當他還是個學生時，他曾在中國參與救濟飢荒的工作，那對他的人生有了很大的改變。他的基金會跟 CERS 都是在 1986 年成立的，由 Avery 頒發補助給想要去中國的人。成功申請到補助的人會經由 James 送到我那裡。他們會打電話給我，詢問怎麼在這些彎曲的泥巴路上找到

Through such connection I got quite used to the parking lot nearby, and the multiple dumpsters around those parking lots. Naturally these dumpsters, an upgrade for my trash, became my next-best friends, after those inside the buildings. Calling this "trashing Caltech" may be anticlimactic now. But it served my purpose quite well at the time.

Caltech however, must not be trashed, as it provided numerous other services to a budding CERS as well. Soon after 1986 and the founding of our organization, other calls started ringing. These were from students, usually grad students, and also from one professor, Dr. James Lee.

James' father, Lee Tsung-Dao, was one of the two Chinese physicists who jointly received the Nobel Prize in 1957. James studied Chinese History and ended up on the faculty of Caltech. Students who took his classes were at times sent over to me if they were interested in Chinese minority regions, my own specialty.

There was also the Durfee Foundation, set up on behalf of R. Stanton Avery who invented self-adhesive labels and went on to found the Avery-Dennison Corporation. In the 1930s, he had a life-changing experience while a student doing famine-relief work in China. The Foundation, set up in the same year as CERS in 1986, provided grants to students of schools attended by Avery who would like to visit China today. Successful applicants were at times sent by

我的木屋。

有兩位被送到我這裡的人，他們不只找到我，後來也留在 CERS 工作。Dr. Pamela Logan 是位雷射光學家，後來在 UCLA 當教授。1990 年代她是我們西藏喇嘛寺廟保護項目的經理。後來，Pam 自己成立一個專注在西藏的非營利組織。

透過 James Lee 和 Durfee 基金會我認識了畢蔚林博士。他的第一次中國經驗是跟著我去的，1987 年他進入中國研究瀕臨絕種的長臂猿，那趟旅程，開啟了畢博士一輩子的志業，在亞洲研究保育野生動物。那時候他已經取得博士學位正在 Caltech 做博士後研究。CERS 怎麼將畢博士從研究室帶到中國的經過不需多說，他長期以來都是 CERS 的董事，而最近更成為研究／項目主任。

Martin Ruzek 來自威斯康辛州的 Green Bay，我的母校也在同一州。他在 Caltech 修了兩個學位之後才到美國航空總署的噴射推進實驗室擔任研究員。由 Caltech 管理的 NASA JPL，大約有五千多名的科學家和工程師。

我因為太空雷達的關係而認識了 Martin，此雷達又稱 Shuttle Imaging Radar-A 或 SIR-A。1981 年太空梭在第二

James to my doorstep, after calling to find out how to drive up the windy, dirt road to my cabin.

Two such candidates not only succeeded in tracking me down, but stayed on later and worked for CERS. Dr. Pamela Logan was a scientist studying laser optics, and later became a professor at UCLA. She became a CERS project manager in the 1990s for our Tibetan monastery conservation projects. Later, Pam went on to start her own NGO focused on Tibetan areas.

I met Dr. Bill Bleisch through James Lee and the Durfee Foundation. His first trip to China with me was in 1987 to study the endangered gibbons, and it led to a life-long pursuit of research and conservation on wildlife in Asia. Bill was at the time doing his post-doc at Caltech. How CERS derailed his scientific laboratory career and ended with decades in China need no elaboration, as he became a long-time CERS board member, and, more recently, Research and Program Director for CERS.

Martin Ruzek hailed from a farm in Green Bay, Wisconsin, the state of my own alma mater. He took two degrees at Caltech before working at NASA's Jet Propulsion Laboratory (JPL), a space-oriented science behemoth with 5,000 scientists and engineers, administered by Caltech.

I met Martin through my early use of the Space-borne Radar on the Shuttle,

次升空，那年和 1984 年從太空梭所拍攝的影像，成為我在 1985 年為美國國家地理雜誌去探長江源頭的關鍵，那些影像指引我前往那個更長也更具意義的源頭。Martin 是幫助我解讀這些影像最重要的人。

去中國探險一趟通常會花上 3、4 個月，那時 Martin 就會幫忙照顧我山上的木屋。他還幫我的房子裝防風暴窗以及蚊帳。CERS 創立後，Martin 持續參與我們，負責遙感技術及地球科學方面的協助，他也是我們去長江重

Dr Bleisch's first CERS expedition / 畢尉林博士第一次與 CERS 去探險

more properly known as Shuttle Imaging Radar-A or SIR-A. It was flown in 1981 during the second ever Shuttle flight. Images obtained from flights in 1981 and 1984 were crucial in getting me to a longer and more important source of the Yangtze River during my 1985 National Geographic Expedition. Martin was instrumental in helping me understand those images from space.

During my long absence on expedition in China, sometimes up to three or four months, Martin would house-sit for me at the cabin. He even installed storm

Martin next to HM at Yangtze source / 長江源頭 Martin 在 HM 旁

Books and stove in cab / 小屋裡的書和火爐

新定位源頭（2005 年）團隊中的一員，還有湄公河源頭
（2007 年）和黃河源頭（2008 年）。身為 CERS 的主任，
畢博士也都參與了這三個源頭的探勘。

1994 年搬回香港前我跟 Dr. Charles Elachi 見了好幾次面，
他是推動太空雷達並將它部署在太空梭上的重要人物。
Dr. Elachi 來自黎巴嫩，先是 Caltech 的研究生，後來在
那裡當教授，接下來成為美國航空總署噴射推進實驗室
的主任。他最近退休了但是仍繼續在 Caltech 教書。

windows and mosquito netting. Later, after the birth of CERS, Martin stayed
involved, handling our remote sensing and space imaging needs to this day,
including being a member on our important expedition to redefine the source
of the Yangtze (2005), followed by those to the sources of the Mekong (2007)
and Yellow River (2008). Bill, being CERS director, was naturally a member
of all three expeditions.

Before moving to Hong Kong, taking with me the Society in 1994, I also had
many opportunities to meet with Dr. Charles Elachi, who was the critical
force behind the invention of the space-borne radar and its deployment on
the Space Shuttle. Dr. Elachi, originally from Lebanon, was first a graduate
of Caltech and later a professor there, and subsequently served as Director
of JPL for well over a decade. He retired recently but continued his teaching
at Caltech.

Both Caltech and my cabin at Millard Canyon counted heavily for me and for
CERS, especially in our early years of exploring China. At the cabin we held
many board meetings and retreats to shape the mission and future direction
of the organization. The place became the home of our important library
of books and photographs, as well as for our small but constantly growing
collection of artefacts on minorities of China. At several occasions, we hosted
parties, including some for visiting scholars from China.

不管是加州理工學院或者米拉德峽谷的小木屋，對我跟 CERS 同樣具有重要的意義，尤其是當我們剛開始進入中國探險的那幾年。在木屋裡，董事們開了無數次的會議討論學會未來的方向和使命。這木屋也是我們的圖書館，收藏了和中國少數民族相關的文物和照片，藏品雖不多但總是在持續的增加中。我們也曾經在這裡接待過好幾次從中國來訪的學者。

現在每當我到洛杉磯尤其是到 Caltech 附近的帕薩迪納，一大早我都會開車到米拉德峽谷，並且在我熟悉的小路上散步，也會停下來看看這棟咖啡色的木屋，那曾經是我生命的中心，也是 CERS 度過第一個十年的地方。

今晚我與老友 Don Conlan 共進晚餐，他支持 CERS 長達 30 多年了。Don 跟我一樣好久前就把米拉德峽谷的木屋賣了。他問我要去哪裡吃晚餐。「就請你訂 Athenaeum 吧！」我說。那裡是 Caltech 教授們的學院俱樂部。

我已經不在這些崇高的大樓後面倒垃圾了。此刻電視台的轉播車又在此聚集，我們弔念今天在墨西哥地震喪命的人。

Today whenever I visit Los Angeles and in particular Pasadena near Caltech, I drive up early in the morning to Millard Canyon, and walk the same trail I once was so familiar with, stopping by to look up at this brown cabin that was central to my life and to the first decade of the existence of CERS.

Tonight I am having dinner with my old friend Don Conlan, a supporter of CERS for over thirty years. Don, like me, sold his cabin at Millard Canyon long ago. He asked me where I would like to have dinner. "Please make a reservation at the Athenaeum," I said. That is the quiet sanctuary that serves as Faculty Club for the professors of Caltech.

I have long since stopped using the trash dumpsters behind some of those majestic buildings. The TV broadcasting trucks, however, may be around tonight, as we mourn for those who died during the devastating earthquake that hit Mexico earlier today.

Hosting guests at cabin / 在小屋接待賓客

一個圓滿文化保育工作

HAPPY ENDING TO A CULTURAL CONSERVATION INITIATIVE

Shek O, HK – October 13, 2017

一個圓滿文化保育工作 傈僳族的弩弓節

2011 年，也就是六年前，*CERS* 非常迅速地決定了必須尋找方法以好好保存傈僳族傳統的弩弓。這個住在雲南西北白馬雪山的傈僳族，傳統上是獵人也是採集者。但是自從 *1984* 年政府為了保護雲南的金絲猴，而建立了自然保護區之後，傈僳族就被禁止打獵了。世代以來用弩弓打獵是傈僳族的生活也是文化，而這傳統就將逐漸地消失了。

從 *2003* 到 *2010* 年，*CERS* 成功地保存了 *21* 棟傈僳族傳統的木屋。這些好不容易保存下來的建築物必須被妥善利用，於是我們跟當地的村長合作，在 *2011* 年嘗試舉辦一年一次的弩弓節。剛開始的幾年，要招集附近的村民來參加和觀看這活動是有困難的。透過可口可樂中國的一部分贊助，於是我們想辦法讓來參加的人都有獎品可拿，甚至還用獎金來吸引傈僳族們暫時放下工作來參加比賽。

HAPPY ENDING TO A CULTURAL CONSERVATION
INITIATIVE Lisu Crossbow Festival

It was six years ago in 2011 when, out of the blue, CERS decided to find a way
to preserve the traditional use of crossbows by the Lisu people. Since 1984
and the establishment of a nature reserve to protect the Yunnan Snub-nosed
Monkey, the Lisu of Xiangguqing, traditionally a hunter/gatherer people
living in the Baima snow mountains of northwest Yunnan, were no longer
allowed to hunt. But for generations, hunting and the use of crossbows was
tied to the life and cultural identity of the Lisu. Gradually that came to an
end.

With the successful preservation of the first Lisu log houses by CERS between
2003 and 2010, now becoming an ensemble of twenty-one houses, we wanted
to find a way to bring these architectural relics to life. So, with the cooperation
of the local village chief, we ventured to launch a once-a-year crossbow festival
in 2011. In the beginning years, it was somewhat difficult to organize nearby
villagers to commit to come as participants and spectators. Through partial
sponsorship from Coca-Cola China, we were able to offer door prizes, as well
as prize money, to attract the Lisu, both men and women, to take time away

我們將這個比賽慶典的時間安排在夏季，好讓學生以及來到我們中甸中心的實習生有機會可以體驗傈傈族的文化，同時也可以增加參與活動的人數。我們派出 CERS 隊和學生隊，3 人一組。這個節日也因此成為 CERS 實習生課程的重點之一。有幾年我們參與的人數多一些，有幾年少一些；有幾年天氣很好，有幾年天公不作美；但是我們從來沒有間斷過。

每年我們都事先做好 3 支大的弩弓跟幾百支竹箭給參加比賽的人使用。每年我們也都會特別設計製作不同的衣服跟帽子，讓這活動更有專屬的感覺。對某些熱中這個比賽的傈傈族年長的男人來說，這活動讓他們

Young and Old, new and used / 年輕人和長者，新的和舊的

from work to join us and compete.

Each year, we timed the event to be when our summer students and interns were with us at our Zhongdian Tibetan Center. This allowed the students to experience Lisu culture, as well as beefing up the number of participants by forming CERS staff and student teams, with three persons to a team. Every year, this festival became one of the highlights of our internship program. Some years we had more participants, some years less. Some years we had fine weather, other times it rained, but we persisted.

Each year we needed to make in advance three large crossbows and a few hundred bamboo arrows for the participants to use. Each year we also made special shirts and caps to give away so the communal feeling would be

CERS Ladies team / CERS 女生組

回憶起用弩弓打獵的日子，但對年輕的一代來說似乎還差了點。2016 那一年，來的人少了，讓我們開始擔心這個節日的未來。

但是今年 8 月，傈僳族人給了我們一個驚喜。節慶當天有好幾百位附近的傈僳族人前來，其中有好多人還是帶著自己特製的弩弓跟箭前來的。突如其來，這些傈僳族的年輕人終於開始重視與認同自己的文化，身分與內涵。我們帶去的 3 把弩弓幾乎都沒有人用，除了 CERS 人員跟學生之外。

節日很熱鬧，大家在比較也炫耀自己特製的弩弓，甚至連箭的做法都很講究。個人跟團體都這樣的講究，當然分數會比前年高出許多。不過這次來的人並不是為了獎品而來，是為了族人的驕傲和社區的團結。總共有近 40 組參加比賽，厲害的射手還參加了個人比賽。

多年來的辛苦跟堅持終於有了成果，這讓我跟其他的同事感到非常欣慰。看來明年，甚至未來的日子，CERS 可以只是去參加節慶，而不用規劃籌備這活動，因為傈僳族自己的熱情遠遠超過我們這些外人。這個沒有在計畫內的項目，終於找到自己的出路；一個棘

enhanced. There was some enthusiasm, especially among older Lisu men, who used the event to reminisce about their old days of hunting with crossbow, but it seemed the younger generation was slow in catching on. In 2016, we felt the crowd had become smaller and began worrying about the festival's future.

This August, however, we were greatly surprised. On the day of the event, several hundred Lisu people came from all the nearby villages, many of them carrying their own specially made crossbows and arrows. As if out of the blue again, these young Lisu are finally catching on to their own culture, identity and integrity. The three crossbows we made and brought along were hardly used at all, except by the CERS and student teams.

There was a lo ϡ t of commotion during the entire day, as people compared and bragged about their own specially-crafted crossbows. Even the arrows were made to very high specifications. With such careful and personal attention, the scores of both team and individual competitors were much higher than in previous years. This time around it seemed that people did not just come for the prizes, but for the comradery and the feeling of ethnic pride and community unity. In all, there were almost forty team entries, and many of the best archers also separately signed up as individual competitors.

I, as well as all of my colleagues, feel extremely gratified that the years of hard work and perseverance are finally paying off. It seems that next year,

手的計畫，被稍微調整過，最後被好好地執行，並且持續執行。這個項目還沒有結束，我們還是會幫忙張羅。CERS 仍舊希望有一天會達成我們的目標。在台前謝幕，退到幕後去。

Carefully crafted crossbow / 用心製作的弩弓

as well as in future years, CERS can come to the festival as a spectator and competitor alone rather than as an organizer, as the new enthusiasm of the Lisu themselves far surpasses what we can bring to them from the outside. Without planning for it, we have found our exit plan to a project haphazardly conceived, incrementally adjusted, and finally well-executed and appropriately carried on. The project is not ending, only our involvement in the organizing. And the CERS team still hopes to score a bulls-eye someday.

Bull's Eye / 中標

國家圖書館出版品預行編目 (CIP) 資料

文化所思 / 黃效文著.
-- 初版 . -- [新北市]：依揚想亮人文 , 2017.12
面；　公分
ISBN 978-986-93841-5-5（平裝）
1. 遊記　2. 世界地理

719　　　　　　　　　　　　　　　　106023921

文化所思

作者・黃效文 ｜ 發行人・劉鋆 ｜ 責任編輯・王思晴 ｜ 美術編輯・Rene Lo ｜ 翻譯
李建興・依揚想亮人文事業有限公司 ｜ 法律顧問・達文西個資暨高科技法律事務所 ｜
出版社・依揚想亮人文事業有限公司 ｜ 經銷商・聯合發行股份有限公司 ｜ 地址・新
北市新店區寶橋路 235 巷 6 弄 6 號 2 樓 ｜ 電話・02 2917 8022 ｜ 印刷・禹利電子分
色有限公司 ｜ 初版一刷・2017 年 12 月（平裝）｜ ISBN・978-986-93841-5-5 ｜ 定價
400 元 ｜ 版權所有　翻印必究 ｜ Print in Taiwan

依
揚
想
亮 出版書目